THE TITANIC AND THE CITY OF WIDOWS IT LEFT BEHIND

THE FORGOTTEN VICTIMS OF THE FATAL VOYAGE

THE TITANIC AND THE CITY OF WIDOWS IT LEFT BEHIND

THE FORGOTTEN VICTIMS OF THE FATAL VOYAGE

Julie Cook

PEN & SWORD
HISTORY

AN IMPRINT OF PEN & SWORD BOOKS LTD.
YORKSHIRE – PHILADELPHIA

First published in Great Britain in 2020 by
PEN AND SWORD HISTORY
an imprint of
Pen and Sword Books Ltd
Yorkshire – Philadelphia

ISBN 978 1 52675 716 6

Typeset in Times New Roman 11.5/14 by
Aura Technology and Software Services, India
Printed and bound in the UK by TJ International

Pen & Sword Books Ltd incorporates the imprints of Pen & Sword
Archaeology, Atlas, Aviation, Battleground, Discovery,
Family History, History, Maritime, Military, Naval, Politics, Railways,
Select, Social History, Transport, True Crime, Claymore Press,
Frontline Books, Leo Cooper, Praetorian Press, Remember When,
Seaforth Publishing and Wharncliffe.

For a complete list of Pen & Sword titles please contact
PEN & SWORD BOOKS LIMITED
47 Church Street, Barnsley, South Yorkshire, S70 2AS, England
E-mail: enquiries@pen-and-sword.co.uk
Website: www.pen-and-sword.co.uk

Or
PEN AND SWORD BOOKS
1950 Lawrence Rd, Havertown, PA 19083, USA
E-mail: Uspen-and-sword@casematepublishers.com
Website: www.penandswordbooks.com

Contents

Acknowledgements

So many kind, knowledgeable and passionate people have assisted me during the researching and writing of this book. I wish to thank Kate Bohdanowicz for initially seeing something in this idea and securing me a publisher, Pen and Sword History; commissioning editor Jonathan Wright as well as Laura Hirst and Alice Wright at Pen and Sword; copy editor Carol Trow; archivists Joanne Smith and Joe Baldwin at the City Archives in Southampton; Vicky Green at the Maritime and Local History section in Southampton Central Library for her infinite knowledge of all things *Titanic* (and patience when I often couldn't get the newspaper microfilm spools to work); Richard Arthur at Southampton Central Library; Maria Newbery curator at the SeaCity Museum, Southampton; Gordon Sutter, Editor of the *Daily Echo* for kindly allowing me to reprint *Titanic* memorial notices; Tim Stanton at the West Sussex Library Service; David Scott-Beddard at the British *Titanic* Society, and to Brian Ticehurst, who died during the time I was writing this book. Brian's research and painstaking work in ensuring the crew's names, backgrounds and memorials were recorded helped me immensely and I wish I could have met him. To a distant cousin, Sarah Gregson, who shares the same great-grandparents Emily and William and who I met while searching for my great-grandparents' history online, for her help and historical expertise. Importantly, huge thanks to the many modern-day descendants of *Titanic* crew who were kind enough to share their memories, photographs and documents with me; Dave Fredericks, Darren Yearsley, Mike Knowlton, Tony Cove, Lyn Aylett, Elaine Estall, Rhona Mintram, Quentin Hurst, Linda Bentley, Linda Paskins, Kerry Wolf, Lorraine Keys and Cheryl Jensen. Thanks to John McAndrew and the Southampton Heritage Photos page on Facebook, without whom I would not have traced so many descendants of *Titanic* crew. Thank you to my aunt Doreen Duncan, William and

ACKNOWLEDGEMENTS

Emily's granddaughter, for her help in sourcing family photos and for her memories, my cousin Robert Duncan and my sister Natalie Cook, another *Titanic* descendant, for her early proof reads and advice. Finally, I thank my father Derek Cook who isn't around to see this book but who always wanted it written and my husband Cornel and our two children Alexander and Adriana who, during the writing of this book, put up with me living, breathing, eating and sleeping all things *Titanic*.

Introduction

When I remember my childhood, one of my earliest memories is of my father watching the film *A Night to Remember*. I can still see his expression as a great and beautiful ship sank beneath the waves while clipped-accented actors filmed in black and white donned their life jackets. My father would then turn to look at me and say, 'Your great-grandfather died on that ship.' I'd gaze at the now half-submerged vessel on the television, its previously twinkling lights suddenly extinguished, the besuited aristocrats and jewel-bedecked women now crammed into lifeboats, and think with horror how awful it must have been not to make it into one, how cold that icy North Atlantic water must have been ... and how terrifying it would have been to drown in the dark.

My father told me that my great-grandfather had been called William Edward Bessant and he was just 40 when he'd perished on the *Titanic* in 1912. He had worked as a fireman on the great ship. As a young child growing up in the 1980s, I'd thought this meant his role was to put out fires, but my father had explained for the hundredth time that 'fireman' meant something entirely different on a steam ship in 1912. William's job hadn't been to *put out* fires, but to keep them going; to stoke them and shovel coal into the great furnaces that fuelled the ship. It was backbreaking, exhausting, sweltering work. *Titanic* had six boiler rooms, 29 boilers, each with three furnaces. These boilers – and the men who worked like slaves to fuel them – quite literally kept the ship sailing. The men working in the boiler rooms had job titles of fireman, who shovelled coal into the furnaces; coal-trimmers, who moved coal around the bunker in wheelbarrows shovelling coal down chutes to the fireman below; and greasers, who supplied lubricating oil for the equipment. The firemen worked four-hour shifts, eight hours off, in their flannel shirts and trousers. They'd stand in front of searing furnaces where the hot, burning coal would spit out lumps of flying, molten debris.

INTRODUCTION

The heat in the boiler room was intense – around 50 degrees centigrade. The bunkers would have been dark with only the glow of the furnaces for light and dust would have been everywhere. These descriptions alone conjure up a sort of hell. But these men were stoical and hard. They had to be. They were called the Black Gang because they were always covered in soot and coal and were part of the lowliest crew members onboard. Often, the job was done by those from the slums or very poor areas of Southampton or indeed from other cities. You had to be strong, tough. But it wasn't just exhausting work, either. It required precision. The firemen needed to feed the exact amount of coal into the furnaces to keep the ship at the required speed.

William, my ancestor from the Black Gang, hadn't had a hope of surviving that night, my father had told me. 'The Black Gang was invisible,' my father said. 'The rich up in first class must have imagined that ship sailed on its own. It was working-class muscle that kept *Titanic* sailing.' Because William was part of the Black Gang, the rich in first class would never have noticed him. It seems he didn't don a life jacket like those elegant, glamorous characters in *A Night to Remember*. It seems he was not ushered to the safety of a lifeboat. His life, so my father explained, was not worth as much as an aristocrat's. No one knows what happened to his body. His wife Emily was simply told he was lost at sea, his body never found. She was left a widow aged just 38 with five children – three of them six years old and under – to rear alone with no breadwinner. Simply, my great-grandfather vanished in the Atlantic Ocean, leaving my great-grandmother a widow and penniless. In Southampton's *Titanic* exhibition at the SeaCity Museum, there is a wall remembering all the crew on *Titanic*. There are pictures to go with some names. But William's face is blank where his name is listed. There is not even a photograph to put to my great-grandfather's name, just a ghostly silhouette.

Time passed. Interestingly, as I got older and spoke to relatives about the disaster, including my own *Titanic*-obsessed father and his sister, my aunt, a story popped up again and again that made William's story even more interesting, perhaps even more tragic. The story was that one day in 1912, weeks after the tragedy, there was a knock at William's widow's front door. A rich gentleman was there, offering to send Emily's eldest daughter Gladys to private school as thanks. The story goes that this 'thanks' was due to my great-grandfather helping this man to a lifeboat on the *Titanic*. According to the story, amidst the chaos on the ship, this gentleman took a note of William's name and address and promised to help his family when he returned to Britain. Gladys, then 12, was offered this private education much to the envy of the other four children but she decided not to accept it. My aunt told me that the others were miffed as they would have jumped at the chance to go in her place. Sibling squabbling aside, the story now began to haunt me.

The details of William's death had always been upsetting. Who couldn't be moved by someone dying in this way and far too young? But before this, I had only thought of William dying – hopefully quickly and relatively painlessly – that night. Now my imagination began to try and answer questions about that night and also to understand how poor William must have felt. I imagined William and his desire to survive and I began to question what happened to him before he drowned. I imagined him feeling the ship hit the iceberg, then hearing the commotion as the alarm went off, then the voices, the shouts, the screams that the ship was sinking. Was he working then, covered in soot and coal at his furnace in the boiler room? Or was he resting in his bunk with the rest of the Black Gang in the lowest part of the ship, drinking, playing cards, or sleeping? Did he and his mates throw down their shovels, climb the staircases of the listing ship and make it to the top? If he did make it to a lifeboat, what on earth was it that made him give up his place? Perhaps shouts of 'women and children first!' made him change his mind. Perhaps was told to move out of the way of the richer passengers. Or did his own humble knowledge that he was only a lowly fireman, and his life worth far less than others, make him stand aside? Did he watch, shivering on deck, as those first-class people were taken to safety, knowing he would drown and never see Emily and his children again?

The truth was, I had no idea whether William made it to a lifeboat and whether he gave up his place helping another passenger. Since the sinking, so many tales of heroism and sacrifice have been told that it could be just that – a family myth to turn William from lowly Black Gang member to hero. For me, it had always seemed unlikely that the lowliest of male crew members could have grabbed themselves spaces in the lifeboats when there were not enough to go around. But of course, research proved that some firemen and coal trimmers *did* make it to lifeboats. One such coal trimmer, Walter Francis Fredericks, who I since discovered was on the same shift pattern as William, made it to the top and was ordered by officers to row the lifeboat. He did so, rowing passengers and other crew to safety and survived, dying in 1960, aged 69. Other firemen did too. So, if other firemen rowed lifeboats, there was every possibility that William made it to one too with his fellow workers. But if he did give up his place knowing that if he did death was inevitable, why? Or did something else happen? Was he injured as the ship listed and sank? Did he not want to risk getting into a lifeboat because *Titanic* was 'unsinkable'? No one knew.

As the years passed, the world's obsession with the *Titanic* seemed to grow. *A Night to Remember* was a classic but before my time. Then James Cameron's epic blockbuster *Titanic* starring Kate Winslet and Leonardo DiCaprio propelled the doomed vessel back into our collective thoughts. It became the world's tragedy, as well as my own family's. I was 20 when I watched the film at the cinema. It felt so very strange watching the tragedy unfold and knowing that my great-grandfather had died the way many of the actors on-screen were doing before my eyes. I remember hearing – and feeling – the creaking, terrible sound of the ship as it hit the iceberg, split and then sank beneath the waves. From my comfortable red velvet cinema seat, I recalled how my father had described William's fate as hopeless. There is a scene in the film where Winslet and DiCaprio's characters try to run through a boiler room and a soot-covered fireman working there tells them angrily that they cannot enter. It was a tiny reference to the existence of the members of the Black Gang. I left the cinema to the sound of Celine Dion's famous theme song, wondering what my great-grandfather would have thought of this film. Would he have wanted more recognition for how hard their lives had been? I longed to see more of the boiler room, to hear their stories, to know what their lives had been like.

I became a journalist for national newspapers and I devoured articles and books about the doomed ship. But I noticed that films, television adaptations and documentaries all seemed to focus far more on the rich passengers and their fight for survival than the poor who worked on board. Other representations seemed more preoccupied with the splendour of the ship; its décor, its opulence, the mega-rich famous guests quaffing champagne in first class. Some focused purely on conspiracy theories. Even the food was analysed in minute detail. I bought a book which featured the splendid last menus on the *Titanic* served in its Ritz Restaurant along with recipes. I read about the exquisite meals served onboard such as oeufs de caille en aspic et caviar – quail eggs in aspic with caviar – and imagined how those dining in first class on the world's most famous ship must have truly felt rather like Leonardo DiCaprio's character Jack when he shouted that he was 'king of the world!' In contrast, the grim boiler rooms with their greedy, molten furnaces were not glamorous. The exhausted, soot-covered, silent firemen of the Black Gang did not inspire sympathy or the audience's care for the outcome of a character such as Kate Winslet's first-class passenger Rose, or Leonardo DiCaprio's steerage passenger Jack. But as I reflected on this unfairness and became a wife and mother, another affront seemed to rise. My father had often talked of my great-grandfather William. Films and books had at least *referred* to the existence of the firemen and coal trimmers in the bowels of the ship, unseen in the higher, luxurious decks by the super-rich guests.

But there was another voice I felt should be heard but was not. The voice of my great-grandmother – William's wife, Emily.

The films, the books, the world's collective sympathy was for the passengers who died in those icy waters that night. We know all about the famous multi-millionaire John Jacob Astor who died and was extolled as a hero for sacrificing his life for others. We know about Benjamin Guggenheim who famously said he would go down like a gentleman. We know about the incredible story of the Unsinkable Molly Brown who survived. It is right that their stories are known, as it is right that the people from all backgrounds who died should and must be remembered. But what about the ones who didn't die, but instead had to carry on? What about the wives, mothers and children of the working men who perished on the ship? When their breadwinner died, and they were thrown into abject poverty – what happened to them?

I began researching and the idea for this book began to germinate. I made contact with descendants of *Titanic*'s crew, scouring online groups and social media and encountered some incredibly kind people only too eager to share their stories of their ancestors; some who came home, others who did not. I met people whose ancestors would have been colleagues or friends with my great-grandfather William, sharing shift patterns and, no doubt, laughs, hopes and dreams. We too shared memories and laughs, but also sad stories. It was eerie to talk to people who were direct relatives of people who would undoubtedly have worked, talked, played cards and drank with my ancestor. Sadly, my father died many years ago, so I've lost further chances to ask about what he knew of William or Emily. His sister Doreen, now in her 80s, remembers their mother, my grandmother, Florence – who was only six when her father William died – talking about how Emily raised five children on her award from a charity. This charity was the *Titanic* Relief Fund. This national charitable fund raised an enormous £412,000 for the relatives of those who perished. This is the equivalent of just under £39m today, according to the Measuring Worth website calculator, which I have used for all such conversions in this book. My great-grandmother received her share as a fireman's wife, which was gratefully received. But, according to family members, in the early days after William's death she was so destitute that she had still had to take in strangers' washing to earn enough to live on. As for the story of my great-grandfather's bravery and self-sacrifice, my aunt assures me that the story of William either giving up his place in a lifeboat or helping a rich passenger to one is true.

Of *Titanic*'s crew of 908, 549 Southampton crew members died. This is a third of the over 1,500 people who lost their lives on the ship. It was said by many at the time there 'wasn't a street in Southampton' that didn't lose someone. It left the city for many years as a kind of waste ground, an eerie ghost town without the men who would have gone back to work on the ships. It left children without fathers and wives without husbands. Many were working class firemen – like my ancestor William – or coal trimmers, victualling workers or stewards. They were the breadwinners for their families and I always wondered how their women managed to feed and clothe their children when their husbands died. But I also wondered how those women must have *felt*. Fiscal worries aside, how was it to lose a husband or son on that fateful ship? How was it to go from the sheer elation of your husband getting work onboard the world's biggest, most luxurious liner only to find out days later that same 'unsinkable' liner had sunk, and him with it? How was it to be handed out help from the widows' fund, only to be checked regularly afterwards? The *Titanic* Relief Fund appointed a special visitor to ensure the recipients of the charity had lifestyles that were respectable and satisfactory – what was it like to have your life, your home, your family checked over in this way? I wondered, too, what it was it like to have to take in washing to survive or do other menial, exhausting work with no time to grieve or reflect on your loss. Emily received a class G award from the *Titanic* Relief Fund – the lowest class of award given to widows and dependants of firemen, scullions and lower-class stewards. Wives of engineers and officers, by comparison, received more. It seemed it was not just the ship that was divided into first class, second class and steerage but as a grieving widow, your class decided how much money you would receive in your grief. Emily received 12 shillings and sixpence a week from the fund and her children received two shillings and sixpence until they came of age – girls at 18, boys at 16. When most films about the *Titanic* end, their last scenes often depict the survivors carrying on with their lives, desperately grateful to be alive but haunted by the tragedy. But I feel a huge swathe of people have not been recognized in their struggle to survive after *Titanic* sank; the crew's wives and children. Who were they? Where did they live? How did they cope when their only source of income vanished forever? And how did they get over their grief?

This book is to give the working-class widows of the men who died on *Titanic* their voices again.

The voices of the city of widows.

Julie Cook,
2019

A list of the 549 crew from Southampton who lost their lives on *Titanic*

Abbott, Ernest Owen	Pantryman	21
Abrams, William	Fireman	33
Adams, R	Fireman	26
Ahier, Percy Snowden	Steward, 1st class	20
Akerman, Albert	Steward, 1st class	28
Akerman, Joseph Francis	Assistant Pantryman, 1st class	35
Alaria, Baptiste	Assistant Waiter	22
Allan, Robert Spencer	Bedroom Steward	36
Allen, Frederick	Lift Steward, 1st class	17
Allen, George	Scullion	26
Allen, Henry	Fireman	32
Allsop, Alfred Samuel	2nd Electrician	34
Allsop, Frank	Steward, 1st class	41
Anderson, Walter J	Bedroom Steward, 1st class	48
Ayling, Edwin George	Assistant Vegetable Cook	25
Back, Charles Frederick	Assistant Lounge Steward	32
Bagley, Edward Ernest	Steward, 1st Class	31
Bailey, George W	Fireman	46
Baines, Richard	Greaser	54
Bannon, John	Greaser	32
Barker, Reginald Lomond	Second Purser	40

Barlow, Charles	Fireman	30
Barlow, George	Bed Room Steward, 2nd class	36
Barnes, Charles	Fireman	29
Barnes, Frederick	Assistant Baker	37
Barnes, J	Fireman	29
Barratt, Arthur (Archie)	Bell Boy, 1st class	15
Barrett, Frederick William	Fireman	33
Barringer, Arthur William	Steward, 1st class	33
Barrow, Harry	Assistant Butcher	35
Barton, Sidney John	Steward, 3rd class	25
Baxter, Harry Ross	Steward, 3rd class	51
Baxter, Thomas Ferguson	Linen Steward, 1st class	48
Beattie, Joseph	Greaser	35
Bedford, William Barnet	Assistant Cook	31
Beere, William	Kitchen Porter	19
Bell, Joseph	Chief Engineer	51
Bendell, Frank	Fireman	24
Benham, Frederick	Steward, 2nd Class	29
Bennett, George	Fireman	29
Benville, E	Fireman	42
Bessant, Edward Ernest	Baggage Steward, 1st class	31
Bessant, William Edward	Fireman	39
Best, Edwin Alfred	Steward, 1st class	38
Bevis, Joseph Henry	Trimmer	22
Biddlecombe, C	Fireman	33
Biggs, Edward Charles	Fireman	21
Billows, J	Trimmer	20
Bishop, Walter Alexander	Bedroom Steward, 1st class	34
Black, Alexander	Fireman	28
Black, D	Fireman	41
Blackman, H	Fireman	24

Blake, Seaton	Mess Steward	26
Blake, Thomas Henry	Fireman	36
Blaney, James	Fireman	29
Blann, Eustace Horatius	Fireman	21
Blumet, Jean	Plateman	27
Bochatez, Alexis	Assistant Chef	29
Bolhuis, Henri	Larder	27
Bond, William John	Bedroom Steward, 1st class	40
Boothby, W	Bedroom Steward, 2nd Class	36
Boston, William John	Assistant Steward, 1st class	30
Bott, William	Greaser	44
Boughton, Bernard John	Steward, 1st Class	24
Boyd, John	Steward, 1st class	35
Boyes, John Henry (Harry)	Steward, 1st class	33
Bradley, Patrick	Fireman	39
Bradley, T	Able Seaman	29
Bradshaw, J A	Plate Steward, 1st class	43
Brewer, Henry	Trimmer	30
Brewster, George Henry	Bedroom Steward, 1st class	48
Bristow, Robert Charles	Steward 3rd class	31
Brookman, John	Steward 3rd class	27
Brooks, J	Trimmer	25
Broome, Athol Frederick	Verandah Steward, 1st class	30
Brown, John	Fireman	25
Brown, Walter James	Steward, 1st class	36
Brugge, Wessel Adrianus	Fireman	39
Buckley, H E	Assistant Vegetable Cook	34
Bull, W	Scullion	20
Bulley, Henry Ashburnham	Boots steward, 2nd Class	21
Bunnell, Wilfred	Plate Steward, 1st class	20
Burr, Ewart Sydenham	Steward, 1st Class	29

Burroughs, Arthur	Fireman	35
Burton, Edward John (Ted)	Fireman	32
Butt, Robert Henry	Steward, 1st class	22
Butt, William	Fireman	30
Butterworth, Jack	Steward, 1st class	23
Calderwood, Hugh	Trimmer	30
Canner, J	Fireman	40
Carr, Richard Stephen	Trimmer	37
Carter, James	Fireman	46
Cartwright, James Edward	Steward, 1st class	32
Casey, T	Trimmer	38
Casswill, Charles	Saloon Steward	34
Castleman, Edward	Greaser	37
Caunt, William Ewart	Grill Cook	27
Cave, Herbert	Steward, 1st class	34
Cecil, Charles	Steward, 3rd class	20
Charman, John	Steward, 2nd class	25
Cherrett, William Victor	Fireman	25
Chisnall, George Alexander	Boilermaker	32
Chitty, Archibald George	Steward, 3rd class	28
Chitty, George Henry	Assistant Baker	52
Chorley, John	Fireman	25
Christmas, Herbert	Steward, 2nd class	33
Clark, Thomas	Steward, 1st Class	37
Clench, George	Able Seaman	31
Coe, Harry	Trimmer	21
Coleman, Albert Edward	Steward, 1st class	28
Coleman, John	Mess Steward	55
Cook, George	Steward, 1st class	33
Coombs, Augustus Charles	Assistant Cook	39
Cooper, Harry	Fireman	26

Cooper, James	Trimmer	25
Copperthwaite, Albert (Bert)	Fireman	22
Corben, Ernest Theodore	Assistant Printer, 1st class	27
Corcoran, Denny	Fireman	33
Couch, Joseph Henry	Greaser	45
Coutin, Auguste	Entrée	28
Cox, William D	Steward, 3rd class	29
Coy, Francis Ernest George	Junior Assistant 3rd Engineer	26
Crabb, Henry	Trimmer	23
Creese, Henry Philip	Deck Engineer	44
Crisp, Albert Hector	Steward, 1st class	35
Cross, W	Fireman	39
Crovella, Luigi	Assistant Waiter	17
Crumplin, Charles	Bedroom Steward, 1st class	35
Cunningham, B	Fireman	30
Curtis, Arthur	Fireman	25
Dashwood, William George	Steward, 2nd class	19
Davies, Gordon Raleigh	Bedroom Steward, 1st	33
Davies, John J	Extra 2nd Baker	27/28
Davies, Robert J	Steward, 2nd class	26
Davies, Thomas	Leading Fireman	33
Dawson, Joseph	Trimmer	23
Dean, George H	Steward, 2nd class	19
Deeble, Alfred Arnold	Steward	29
Derrett, Arthur	Steward, 1st class	26
Deslandes, Percival Stainer	Saloon Steward, 1st class	36
Dickson, W	Trimmer	36
Dinenage, James Richard	Steward, 1st class	47
Dodd, Edward Charles	Junior 3rd Engineer	37
Dodd, George	Second Steward, 1st class	44

Dodds, Renny [Henry] Watson	Junior Assistant 4th Engineer	27
Dolby, Joseph	Reception Steward, 1st class	35
Donoghue, T	Bedroom Steward, 1st class	35
Dornier, Louis	Assistant Fish Cook	20
Doughty, N	Steward, 2nd class	22
Doyle, Laurence	Fireman	27
Duffy, William Luke	Writer/ Engineer's Clerk	26
Dunford, William	Hospital Steward, 3rd class	41
Dyer, Henry Ryland	Senior Assistant 4th Engineer	24
Dyer, William	Steward, 1st class	31
Eagle, Alfred James	Trimmer	27
Eastman, Charles	Greaser	44
Ede, George B	Steward, 3rd Class	22
Edge, Frederick William	Deck Steward, 2nd class	37
Edwards, Clement	Assistant Pantryman, 1st class	39
Elliott, Everett Edward	Trimmer	24
Evans, George	Steward	33
Evans, George Richard	Steward, 1st Class	32
Evans, William	Trimmer	30
Farquharson, William Edward	Senior 2nd Engineer	39
Fay, Thomas Joseph	Greaser	30
Fellowes, Alfred J	Assistant Boots Steward, 1st class	29
Feltham, G	Vienna Baker	36
Ferrary, Anton	Trimmer	34
Ferris, W	Leading Fireman	38
Finch, Harry	Steward, 3rd class	18
Ford, Ernest	Steward, 3rd class	31
Ford, F	Bed Room Steward, 2nd class	37
Ford, H	Trimmer	22

Ford, Thomas	Leading Fireman	30
Foster, Albert C	Storekeeper	37
Franklin, Alan	Steward, 2nd class	29
Fraser, J	Fireman	30
Fraser, James	Junior Assistant 3rd Engineer	29
Freeman, Edward Ernest Samuel	Deck Steward, 1st class	43
Gatti, Luigi	Manager	36
Geddes, Richard Charles	Bedroom Steward, 1st class	31
Geer, Alfred Ernest	Fireman	24
Gilardino, Vincenzo Pio	Waiter	31
Giles, John	2nd Baker	30
Gill, Joseph Stanley	Bedroom Steward, 1st class	34
Gill, Thomas Patrick	Ship's Cook	38
Golder, M W	Fireman	32
Gollop, F	Assistant Passenger Cook	28
Gordon, J	Trimmer	29
Goree, Frank	Greaser	42
Goshawk, Arthur James	Third Saloon Steward, 1st class	31
Gosling, Bertram James	Trimmer	22
Gosling, S	Trimmer	26
Gradidge, Ernest Edward	Fireman	22
Green, George	Trimmer	20
Gregory, David	Greaser	40
Gumery, George	Mess Steward	24
Gunn, Joseph Alfred	Steward, 2nd class	28
Gwinn, William Logan	Postal Clerk	37
Hall, F A J	Scullion	38
Hall, J	Fireman	32
Hallett, George	Fireman	22
Hamblyn, Ernest William	Bed Room Steward, 2nd class	41

Hamilton, Ernest W	Assistant Smoke Room Steward, 1st class	25
Hands, Bernard	Fireman	53
Hannam, George	Fireman	27
Harding, Alfred John	Assistant Pantryman, 2nd class	20
Harris, Amos Fred	Trimmer	21
Harris, Charles	Steward	18
Harris, Clifford	Bell Boy, 1st class	16
Harris, Edward	Fireman	28
Harrison, Norman	Junior 2nd Engineer	38
Hart, James	Fireman	49
Harvey, Herbert Gifford	Junior Assistant 2nd Engineer	30
Haslin, James	Trimmer	45
Hatch, Hugh	Scullion	22
Hawkesworth, James	Steward, 2nd class	38
Hawkesworth, William Walter	Assistant Steward, 1st class	43
Hayter, Arthur	Bedroom Steward, 1st class	44
Head, A	Fireman	24
Hendy, Edward Martin	Steward, 1st class	38
Hensford, Herbert George	Assistant Butcher	29
Hill, Henry Parkinson	Steward, 3rd class	36
Hill, James	Trimmer	25
Hill, James Colston (Jimmie)	Bedroom Steward, 1st class	38
Hinckley, George	Bath Steward, 2nd class	35
Hinton, Stephen William	Trimmer	30
Hiscock, Sidney George	Plate Steward, 1st class	22
Hoare, Leonard James (Len)	Steward, 1st class	18.5
Hodge, Charles (Charley)	Senior Assistant 3rd Engineer	28
Hodges, W	Fireman	26
Hodgkinson, Leonar d	Senior 4th Engineer	45

Holloway, Sidney	Assistant Steward, 1st class	20
Holman, Harry	Able Seaman	27
Hopgood, Roland	Fireman	29
Hopkins, Fred	Plate Steward, 1st class	16
Hosgood, Richard	Fireman	22
Hosking, George Fox	Senior 3rd Engineer	36
House, William (Jack)	Steward, 1st class	38
Howell, Arthur Albert	Steward, 1st class	31
Hughes, William Thomas	Assistant 2nd Steward, 1st class	33
Humby, Frederick	Plate Steward, 2nd class	16
Humphreys, Humphrey	Steward, 2nd class	31
Hunt, Tom	Fireman	28
Hurst, Charles John (Jack)	Fireman	35
Hutchinson, John Hall	Joiner	26
Hutchison, James	Vegetable Cook	29
Ide, Harry John	Bedroom Steward, 1st class	32
Ingram, G	Trimmer	21
Ingrouille, Henry	Steward, 3rd class	21
Ings, William Ernest	Kitchen Porter	20
Instance, T	Fireman	33
Jackson, Cecil (Jack)	Assistant Boots Steward, 1st class	22
Jacopson, John	Trimmer	29
Jago, Joseph	Greaser	27
James, Thomas	Fireman	27
Janaway, William Frank	Bedroom Steward, 1st class	35
Jarvis, Walter	Fireman	37
Jeffery, William Alfred	Controller	28
Jenner, Harry	Saloon Steward, 2nd class	41
Jensen, Charles Valdemar	Steward, 2nd class	25
Joas, N	Fireman	38
Johnstone, Harry	Assistant Ship's Cook	26

Jones, Albert (Bert)	Steward, 2nd class	17
Jones, Arthur Ernest	Plate Steward, 2nd class	38
Jones, H	Roast Cook	29
Jones, Reggie	Steward, 1st class	20
Jouannault, Georges	Assistant Sauce Cook	24
Jukes, James	Greaser	35
Jupe, Boylett Herbert	Assistant Electrician	31
Kearl, Charles Henry	Greaser	43
Kearl, G	Trimmer	24
Keegan, James	Leading Fireman	38
Kelland, Thomas	Library Steward, 2nd class	21
Kelly, James	Greaser	44
Kemp, Thomas Holman	Extra Assistant 4th Engineer	43
Kenchenton, Frederick	Greaser	37
Kennel, Charles	Hebrew Cook	30
Kenzler, August	Storekeeper	43
Kerr, Thomas (Tommy)	Fireman	26
Ketchley, Henry	Steward, 1st class	30
Kieran, James W	Chief 3rd Class Steward	32
Kieran, Michael	Storekeeper	31
King, Alfred	Lift Steward, 1st class	18
King, G	Scullion	20
Kingscote, William Ford	Steward, 1st class	43
Kinsella, L	Fireman	30
Kirkham, J	Greaser	39
Kitching, Arthur Alfred	Steward, 1st class	30
Klein, Herbert	Barber, 3rd class	33
Lake, William	Steward, 1st class	35
Lane, Albert Edward	Steward, 1st class	34
Lawrence, Arthur	Assistant Second Steward, 1st class	35

Leader, Archie	Confectioner	22
Lee, H	Trimmer	18
Lefeuvre, George	Steward, 1st class	32
Levett, George	Assistant Pantryman, 1st class	21
Light, Christopher William	Fireman	21
Light, W	Fireman	47
Lloyd, Humphrey	Steward, 1st class	32
Lloyd, W	Fireman	29
Locke, A	Scullion	33
Long, F	Trimmer	28
Long, William	Trimmer	30
Lovell, John	Grill Cook	38
Lydiatt, Charles	Steward, 1st class	38
Lyons, William Henry	Able Seaman	26
Mabey, John C.	Steward, 3rd class	24
Mackie, George William	Bed Room Steward, 2nd class	34
Major, Thomas Edgar	Bath Steward, 1st class	35
Mantle, Roland Frederick	Steward, 3rd class	36
March, John Starr	Postal Clerk	48
Marks, John	Assistant Pantryman, 1st class	26
Marrett, G	Fireman	22
Marriott, John William	Assistant Pantryman, 1st class	20
Marsh, Frederick Charles	Fireman	39
Maskell, Leopold Adolphus	Trimmer	25
Mason, J	Leading Fireman	39
Matherson, David	Able Seaman	30
Mathias, Montague Vincent	Mess Steward	27
Mattman, Adolf	Iceman	21
Maxwell, John	Carpenter	31
May, Arthur	Fireman	23

May, Arthur William	Fireman Messman	60
Mayo, William Peter	Leading Fireman	27
Maytum, Alfred	Chief Butcher	52
McAndrew, Thomas	Fireman	36
McCarthy, Frederick J	Bedroom Steward, 1st class	36
McCastlin, W	Fireman	38
McElroy, Hugh Walter	Purser	37
McGarvey, Edward Joseph	Fireman	34
McGaw, Erroll V	Fireman	30
McGrady, James	Steward, 1st class	27
McGregor, J	Fireman	30
McMicken, Benjamin Tucker	Second Pantryman Steward, 1st class	21
McMullin, James	Steward, 1st class	32
McRae, William Alexander	Fireman	30
Mellor, Arthur	Steward, 1st class	34
Milford, George	Fireman	29
Mintram, William	Fireman	46
Mishellany, Abraham	Printer	52
Mitchell, Lawrence	Trimmer	18
Moore, Alfred Ernest	Steward, 2nd class	39
Moores, Richard Henry	Greaser	44
Morgan, Arthur Herbert	Trimmer	27
Morgan, Thomas A	Fireman	26
Morrell, R	Trimmer	21
Morris, Arthur	Greaser	30
Morris, W	Trimmer	24
Moss, William	First Saloon Steward, 1st class	34
Muller, L	Interpreter & Steward, 3rd class	36
Mullin, Thomas	Steward, 3rd class	20
Murdoch, William McMaster	First Officer	38

Nettleton, G	Fireman	28
Newman, Charles Thomas	Asssistant Storekeeper	32
Nicholls, Sidney	Steward, 1st class	39
Nichols, Alfred	Boatswain	42
Nichols, Arthur D	Steward, 3rd class	34
Noon, John	Fireman	35
Norris, James	Fireman	23
Noss, Bertram Arthur	Fireman	21
Olive, Charles	Greaser	31
Olive, Ernest Roskelly	Clothes Presser, 1st class	28
O'Loughlin, William Francis Norman	Surgeon	62
Orpet, Walter	Steward, 1st class	31
Orr, J	Assistant Vegetable Cook	40
Osborne, William	Steward, 1st class	32
Owen, Lewis	Steward, 2nd class	43
Pacey, Reginald Ivan	Lift Steward, 2nd class	17
Pachera, Jean Baptiste Stanislas	Assistant Larder	20
Paice, Richard Charles John	Fireman	32
Painter, Charles	Fireman	31
Painter, Frank	Fireman	29
Paintin, James Arthur	Captain's Steward	29
Parsons, Edward	Chief Storekeeper	37
Parsons, Frank Alfred	Senior Fifth Engineer	26
Parsons, Richard	Steward, 2nd class	18
Pearce, Alfred Ernest	Steward, 3rd class	24
Pedrini, Ales.	Assistant Waiter	21
Penny, William Farr	Steward, 2nd class	30
Penrose, John Poole	Bedroom Steward, 1st class	49
Perkins, Laurence Alexander	Telephone Operator	22

Perrin, William Charles	Boots steward, 2nd class	39
Perriton, Hubert Prowse	Steward, 1st class	31
Perry, Henry	Trimmer	23
Petty, Edwin Henry	Bed Room Steward	25
Phillips, George	Greaser	27
Phillips, Walter John	Store Keeper	35
Pitfield, William James	Greaser	25
Platt, W	Scullion	18
Poggi, Emilio	Waiter	26
Pond, George	Fireman	32
Pook, Percy Robert	Assistant Pantryman, 2nd class	34
Porteus, Thomas	Assistant Butcher	32
Preston, Thomas Charles Alfred	Trimmer	20
Proctor, Charles	Chef	40
Proudfoot, Richard	Trimmer	23
Pryce, Charles William	Steward,1st class	24
Pugh, Percy	Leading Fireman	31
Pennal, Thomas Frederick	Bath Steward	33
Pusey, John E	Steward, 1st class	35
Randall, Frank Henry	Steward, 2nd class	29
Rattenbury, William Henry	Assistant Boots Steward, 1st class	38
Read, J	Trimmer	21
Reed, Charles S	Bed Room Steward, 2nd class	43
Reeves, F	Fireman	31
Reid, R	Trimmer	30
Revell, William James Francis	Steward, 1st class	31
Rice, Percy	Steward, 3rd class	19
Richards, Joseph James	Fireman	29
Rickman, George Albert (Will)	Fireman	36

Ricks, Cyril George	Storekeeper	23
Ridout, W	Steward, 2nd class	29
Rimmer, Gilbert	Steward, 1st class	27
Roberts, Robert George	Fireman	35
Roberton, George Edward	Steward, 2nd class	19
Robinson, James William	Steward, 1st class	30
Rogers, Edward James William	Storekeeper	32
Rous, Arthur J	Plumber	26
Rowe, Edward M	Steward, 1st class	31
Rudd, Henry	Assistant Storekeeper	23
Russell, Boysie Richard	Steward, 2nd class	16
Rutter, Sidney Frank	Fireman	27
Ryan, Thomas	Steward, 3rd class	27
Samuel, Owen Wilmore	Steward, 2nd class	41
Sangster, Charles	Fireman	32
Saunders, D E	Steward, 1st class	26
Saunders, F	Fireman	22
Saunders, W	Fireman	23
Saunders, Walter Edward	Trimmer	25
Sawyer, Robert James	Window Cleaner	30
Scott, Archibald	Fireman	40
Scott, John	Assistant Boots Steward, 1st class	21
Scovell, Robert	Steward, 2nd class	42
Sedunary, Sidney Francis	Second 3rd Class Steward	25
Self, Alfred Henry	Greaser	38
Shea, John	Steward, 1st class	39
Shea, Thomas	Fireman	32
Shepherd, Jonathan	Junior Assistant 2nd Engineer	30
Shillabeer, Charles Frederick	Trimmer	20
Siebert, Sidney Conrad	Steward, 1st class	29

Simmons, Frederick C	Steward, 1st class	27
Simmons, William	Passenger Cook	32
Skeates, W	Trimmer	26
Skinner, Edward	Steward, 1st class	33
Slight, Harry John	Steward, 3rd class	34
Slight, William H	Larder Cook	35
Sloan, Peter	Chief Electrician	31
Small, William	Leading Fireman	40
Smillie, John (Jack)	Steward, 1st class	29
Smith, Charles	Kitchen Porter	38
Smith, Charles (Charley)	Bed Room Steward, 2nd class	38
Smith, Edward John	Captain	62
Smith, Ernest George	Trimmer	26
Smith, F	Assistant Pantryman, 1st class	20
Smith, James Muil	Junior 4th Engineer	35
Smith, James William	Assistant Baker	24
Smith, John Richard Jago	Postal Clerk	35
Smith, Robert G	Steward, 1st class	30
Smith, William	Able Seaman	26
Smither, Henry James	Fireman	22
Snellgrove, G	Fireman	40
Snooks, W	Trimmer	26
Stafford, Michael	Greaser	37
Stagg, John Henry (Jack)	Steward, 1st class	37
Stanbrook, Alfred Augustus	Fireman	30
Stebbings, Sydney Frederick	Chief Boots	34
Steel, Robert Edward	Trimmer	27
Stocker, H	Trimmer	20
Stone, Edmund J	Bedroom Steward, 1st class	33
Stone, Edward Thomas	Bedroom Steward, 2nd class	29

Stroud, Edward Alfred Orlando	Steward, 2nd class	19
Stroud, Harry John	Steward, 1st class	33
Strugnell, John	Steward, 1st class	30
Stubbings, Harry Robert	2nd Class Cook	29
Stubbs, James Henry	Fireman	28
Sullivan, S	Fireman	28
Swan, W	Bedroom Steward, 1st class	46
Symonds, J	Steward, 1st class	38
Talbot, George Frederick	Steward, 3rd class	21
Tamlyn, Frederick	Mess Steward	23
Taylor, C	Able Seaman	35
Taylor, Cuthbert	Steward, 3rd class	26
Taylor, F	Fireman	42
Taylor, Frederick	Fireman	23
Taylor, William John	Steward, 1st class	30
Terrell, Bertram	Seaman	22
Teuton, Thomas	Steward, 2nd class	32
Thomas, Joseph	Fireman	25
Thompson, Herbert Henry	Storekeeper	25
Thorley, William	Assistant Cook	39
Tietz, Carlo	Kitchen Porter	27
Tizard, Arthur	Fireman	31
Topp, Thomas	2nd Butcher	28
Toshack, James	Steward, 1st class	31
Tozer, James	Greaser	30
Turley, Richard	Fireman	35
Turner, L	Steward, 1st class	28
Veal, Arthur	Greaser	34
Veal, Thomas Henry Edom	Steward, 1st class	38
Vear, Henry	Fireman	32

Vear, William	Fireman	33
Wake, Percy	Assistant Baker	37
Wallis, Catherine Jane	Matron, 2nd class	35
Walpole, James	Chief Pantryman Steward, 1st class	48
Walsh, Katherine	Stewardess, 1st class	32
Ward, Edward	Bedroom Steward, 1st class	34
Ward, J	Leading Fireman	31
Ward, Percy Thomas	Bedroom Steward, 1st class	38
Wardner, Frederick Albert	Fireman	39
Wareham, Robert Arthur	Bedroom Steward, 1st class	36
Wateridge, Edward Lewis	Fireman	25
Watson, W	Fireman	27
Weatherstone, Thomas Herbert	Steward, 1st class	24
Webb, Brooke Holding	Smoke Room Steward, 1st class	50
Webb, S	Trimmer	28
Webber, Francis Albert (Frank)	Leading Fireman	31
Welch, H	Assistant Cook	23
White, Frank Leonard	Trimmer	28
White, J	Glory Hole Steward, 3rd class	27
White, Leonard Lisle Oliver	Steward, 1st class	32
Whitford, Alfred Henry	Steward, 2nd class	39
Williams, Samuel Solomon	Fireman	26
Williamson, James Bertram	Postal Clerk	35
Willis, W	Steward, 3rd class	46
Wilson, Bertie	Senior Assistant 2nd Engineer	28
Wilton, William	Trimmer	45
Willsher, William Audrey	Assistant Butcher	33

Witt, Harry Dennis	Fireman	39
Wittman, Henry	Bedroom Steward, 1st class	34
Wood, Henry	Trimmer	30
Woodford, Frederick	Greaser	40
Woody, Oscar Scott	Postal Clerk	44
Wormald, Frederick Henry	Steward, 1st class	36
Wrapson, Frederick Bernard	Assistant Pantryman, 1st class	19
Wyeth, James	Fireman	25
Young, Frank	Fireman	30
Zarrachi, L	Wine Butler	26

Prologue

As she ran through the streets of Southampton, Emily Bessant ignored the wet feeling in her boots as she splashed through the puddles caused by April rain. She heaved her two-year-old Albert higher up on her hip as she struggled on, calling out to her other four children – Charles, 15, Gladys, 12, Florence, six, and Leonard, four – to keep up.

They'd been rushing through the streets of Southampton for over an hour. It was a two-and-a-half mile walk from her home in Henry Road to Canute Road where the White Star Line offices were at Southampton Docks.

She might have caught the tram part of the way, had she had the money. But in any case, the city was heaving with people today. The normally quiet streets of Southampton – where poor but house-proud women scrubbed their doorsteps and chatted over the garden fence – were chaos.

Now wives were running from their houses to their neighbours, their aprons still on, baking left unfinished, children screaming, toddlers and babies blissfully unaware, mothers sobbing that their sons were lost at sea.

Emily hurried on and didn't notice her wet stockings anymore. Her head was pounding and her heart thudding. The sweat that coursed down her back under her dress and corset, the moans of her children to slow down, the pain in her feet, the ache in her arms from carrying Albert, were nothing.

Only one refrain reeled in her head: Let his name be on the survivors' list…let his name be there…

When she reached the docks, though, she could no longer move for people. There were hundreds there, waiting, shuffling forward, trying to get closer.

Without looking, she reached out for the hands of the younger children, calling out to the older ones to make sure they stay close in the crowd.

'Stay near!' she yelled, jostling past young boys carrying placards from the local paper, the *Southern Daily Echo*.

Those placards featured a picture of that wretched ship, the ship they'd been able to see for miles while it had docked before it sailed from Southampton port, with its tall funnels that towered over the terraced streets of Southampton, like some ungodly thing; that ship they'd all said was unsinkable.

Emily wouldn't look at that image now. She wouldn't think about it. She ignored the cries of the Echo boys: *Titanic* sinks!

She stood behind the hundreds of other wives, mothers, sisters and brothers and waited. Her husband William had been at sea before on the ship the *Oceanic*.

He'd come back then.

He'd come back now.

All around Emily, women like her stood with the same expressions on their faces. Men, too, had gathered; fathers of sons who'd taken a job on the *Titanic*, brothers, uncles. Many had taken work on the ship despite never having been at sea before.

William had been at sea a year earlier on the liner the *Oceanic*. He'd been a fireman – a member of the notorious, soot-covered Black Gang. It was backbreaking, exhausting, roasting work. Men worked in their flannel trousers and shirts for four hours at a time without stopping.

William had complained of the long hours to Emily, but he was used to it, having worked on ships before. So, he had readily signed up at the last minute with just days to go when the White Star Line had announced they were recruiting more men from Southampton. Indeed, when William had been taken on as a fireman, Emily had celebrated. His wages would be £6 a month.

It meant he'd be away for weeks but meant the family would eat.

Many other seafaring men had pawned their best shoes so they could leave their wives with some money to live off while they were on the *Titanic*.

Now Emily shuffled forward, still holding Albert in her arms, still checking her other four children were close by in a crowd that was growing not only in size but, now, in tension.

Now, people began to call out.

Where's the list?

Are there any survivors?

All Emily could do was wait her turn to reach the front; to see the survivors' list and check William's name was on it. He was 40; too young to drown. They'd married almost 20 years earlier when Emily had been 19 and William 22. They'd been together too long for this horror to be true.

Emily closed her eyes and prayed his name would be on that list. But as she did, several women she recognised from streets she knew walked past her back from the docks, sobbing, holding each other up, some unable to stand.

Their men had been firemen too. Or stewards. Or scullions.

Emily felt her damp boots again and suddenly thought of all the pairs of best shoes in the pawn shops that would never see their wearers again.

Chapter 1

Chance of a Lifetime

If you could jump into a time machine and travel back to April 1912 and if you walked to certain points of the terraced streets in Southampton city centre, dodged the mucky-faced children playing in the streets and peered over the rows of hanging laundry, you would be able to see it. From miles around the city, in fact, the great ship could be seen. At 269 metres long and 32 metres high, *Titanic* towered like a giant on the Southampton skyline, its bright yellow funnels visible to all, like some futuristic invader. To the poor living in Southampton, the arrival of this majestic vessel – the biggest and most opulent ship ever built – brought waves of excitement and, more importantly, hope. Those bright yellow funnels didn't just represent the power of the steam ship age. Those sky-skimming funnels represented jobs – jobs as stewards, firemen, coal trimmers, victualing workers, engineers. To the poor they represented the chance to put food on the table. The White Star Line, which also operated the mega ships of the day RMS *Olympic* and RMS *Oceanic*, had set up offices in Southampton in 1907 and now Southampton would be a rival to great ports such as Liverpool and London. It meant the city's docks would be able to berth ever larger ships and was about to become gateway to the world.

It is fair to say that, for the poor, life that year was grim and far more about survival than living. In the February of 1912, coal miners had called a national coal strike with an aim of securing a minimum wage. It lasted 37 days – in a cold winter – and caused enormous disruption to shipping schedules. In a world of ships powered by steam, coal was its lifeblood. Without it, ships remained in dock, unable to sail. As a result, workers were laid off. And in a city like Southampton where jobs were scarce unless a man went to sea, it had a devastating effect on employment. Southampton then had a population of 119,000 and there were 17,000 unemployed. Even if a man did have work, life was a hard, often miserable existence, with the only punctuation to the mundanity a visit to the local pub, if you had enough money. Working class families lived in poor areas of the city such as Northam and Chapel, situated on the west bank of the river Itchen which branches off from the waters of the Solent. The vicinity of Northam and Chapel to the docks meant it was the assumed destiny of many men born there to work on the ships. But the tiny, dark terraced houses often housed upwards of eight people in cramped conditions. Situated near the grim slaughter houses and a margarine factory, the streets were prone to flooding and the ground floors of houses were often destroyed by rising water levels. As one unnamed person, whose father was a coal porter, recalled in the book *Chapel and Northam: An Oral History of Southampton's Dockland Communities 1900-1945*:

> 'Always the men were out of work, especially in Chapel. My dad was a Coal Porter, he used to coal the ships. There weren't many people had permanent jobs then - it was casual. You were picked up one day and dropped the next...I don't know how we used to live, to tell you the truth.[1]

Another interviewee, who spoke in 1984 for the Southampton Museum Oral History Archive, recalled, 'Times were bad for boys in Southampton in those days, in the 1910s so the brigade was started here.'

The brigade he speaks of is the Gordon Boys, the city's messengers. The boys would do all sorts of jobs and tasks from helping to carry elderly people upstairs, delivering food or parcels, even running back to the local newspaper with the football scores at half time. It was a job that young, poor boys from the 'low-born' areas of Northam and Chapel often took on. Children, on the whole, left school at 14 and being a member of the Gordon Boys was the only things a child could get to earn some money. Another interviewee for the Archive said, 'Everyone was poor.'

Poverty, especially after the coal strike, was indeed everywhere and not just in Southampton. London felt the pinch and even when the strike ended, it was recorded that 'the distress it has caused continues. Prices are up and the distress in the poor areas of London is acute'.[2]

Indeed, the coal strike meant that men eager for work would go down to the docks knowing the chance of actually gaining any paid work was slim. If work was available, the men would then take turns taking a day's work with other seamen. 'At the Dock Station now about forty men of all grades – guards, porters, shunters etc – are "stood down" and men taking turns a day at a time at "resting".' This was to 'distribute the burden of unemployment equally over the whole staff.'[3]

William would no doubt have stood down every few days, to share what work there was with his colleagues. Whether he was helping distribute the burden of unemployment or not, it must have caused friction in a household with seven mouths to feed. Women such as my great-grandmother Emily would have had to make their husband's meagre, on-off wages go even further with prices rising. Add to that the fact wives had to tolerate their husbands sharing work with other men, and I imagine there would have been many rows behind closed doors. While men roamed the streets for work, women barely left the house, such was their domestic workload. The houses of the working class still didn't have electricity and washing was often done in a tin bath and then dried in the back garden. Dinner would have been simple, hearty, calorific food like bread and dripping or bread and margarine – or whatever you could get your hands on. My father told me as a child that his mother, Emily's daughter, remembered wolfing down whatever they were given because 'you never knew when you'd eat again.' This happened in many other families too. One interviewee, known only as 'MG', recalled this life in an oral history interview for Southampton Oral History Project and recounted that stale cakes would have always been gratefully received. '...a penny worth of stale cakes and [we] used to have that and we, and we were satisfied with it yer know. We never said oh yer know, not like the nippers now. Oh, I ain't eating that, yer know. If you didn't eat it, you went without.'

My great-grandmother Emily Bessant would also have known about the need to eat what was affordable or go without. Waste would have been an alien concept. She, William and their five children lived in a terraced two-up, two-down in Henry Road, Freemantle – a part of Southampton which was then considered more of a suburb rather than the city proper. It was not as poor an area as the dockside areas of Northam and Chapel where most seafaring families lived but life still would have been tough looking after Charles, then 15, Gladys, 12, Florence, my grandmother, then aged six, and Leonard, four, and two-year-old Albert. A sixth had died as a baby. Emily and William were certainly prolific at producing offspring. My aunt Doreen told me, 'My mother said she wondered when

Emily would stop having children.' It is true that my great-grandmother was almost perpetually pregnant during her marriage, perhaps at least showing that there was affection and love between her and William. But large families were common at a time when many families lost a child or even more to illness or disease.

My great-grandfather had been born to farm labourer parents out of wedlock in a rural village called Eling, five miles away from Southampton city centre. Coming to work and live in the city with an ever-growing, bustling port would have been his way out. Farm labouring and work in agriculture was being ever replaced by machinery and imported meats and other foodstuffs from abroad. The docks and the boats offered him a new opportunity. In 1912, William was 40 and an old hand on steam ships. He had worked previously as a fireman on the vessel the RMS *Oceanic*, also a White Star Line ship. He had also worked as a labourer for the Union Castle Line, a steam shipping company that transported coal from Wales to Southampton. Ships were William's second home, so when word spread that the White Star Line needed men to work on its newest vessel, the biggest and most technologically-advanced ship ever built at the time, William would have seen this as the opportunity of a lifetime to earn for his family and give them a few more weeks' breathing space from money worries. But William should not have had a job on *Titanic* at all, my aunt Doreen explained to me. The ship already had its crew men for the boiler rooms, employing workers from Belfast where the ship had been built and from where it had originally set sail. However, fate would play its role in leading my great-grandfather to his doomed destiny. The ship suffered a fire in one of its boiler rooms before she even left Belfast. This fire was mentioned in the official inquiry in 1912. As a result, some crew from Belfast refused to sail and gave up their positions on *Titanic*. It freed up jobs once the ship arrived in Southampton. 'Granddad wasn't even meant to go,' my aunt Doreen told me. 'He heard there were jobs going because some of the crew from Ireland had refused to sail after the fire.' It meant there was a job spare for my great-grandfather. Simply, it was the chance of a lifetime. *Titanic* was the largest manmade object on the planet. She was also the most opulent. William had sailed on large steam ships and the chance to take a job on board *Titanic*, even at the eleventh hour, would have been like scooping up a winning lottery ticket. With a wife and five children to feed, William would have been under constant pressure to seek work – and *keep* work.

For Emily, her role as the wife of a seafaring man would have been like that of any other woman of her class; to rear children, to keep house, to cook and feed the family, albeit on a meagre, sometimes non-existent budget. As working class, she would have had minimal rights; it would be another six years before women won the right to vote and then only if they were homeowners. The street where she lived would have housed families tightly packed, cheek-by-jowl, in similar terraced houses. Laundry hung in the streets, women scrubbed their front door steps while their children played outside, skipping or chasing a ball or hoop while trying to ignore the ever-present, unrelenting gnaw of hunger in their stomachs. This is not an exaggeration. Children were hungry, some starving. The cost of the national coal strike earlier in 1912 to women like Emily and her children would have been immense. Dockers and seamen who were already only casually employed would be laid off – without coal, no ships were sailing. Thousands died that year from hypothermia and nationally over one million were out of work. The poverty, of course, affected the most vulnerable. In one of the city's schools, Northam Girls' School, their log book in March 1912 has the following entry: 'Twenty-two free meals given today. The distress is daily becoming more acute, owing to stagnation caused by the coal strike.'

Children went to school hungry while their fathers wandered around looking for work that often never materialized. Men queued daily at Southampton docks to ask about work even if no jobs were advertised. If there was work, men sometimes had to quite literally fight for it, as one interviewee recalled of the time: 'I used to fight for a job in the docks. Used to fight for half a day there, and when I say fight, I mean fight.'[4] Hunger must have burned in their stomachs and, in turn, had a detrimental effect on their health. In fact, in 1900, 40 per cent of the recruits who tried to enter the British Army were rejected. The reason was ill health. Working class people were malnourished, thin, and hungry. Their children would have been the same. Signing on to serve on the *Titanic* was more than just another job opportunity, it was a godsend and meant a man could feed his children.

In the Bessant household, Emily did not work. There were, of course, jobs advertized in abundance for women in service, for seamstresses, dressmakers, domestic cooks but men here were the breadwinners. And if Sheffield had steel, Southampton had its docks. But it was a hard life for the men; a life of physical endurance, of long days and calloused hands and empty stomachs. No wonder, then, that many of the Black Gang were known for their rough and ready behaviour and heavy drinking, as Richard P. De Kerbrech writes in his account of life as a Black Gang member, 'Firemen and trimmers were a tough breed and needed careful supervision.'[5]

But perhaps the heavy drinking was the only thing to numb the hunger and help them, for a while at least, to forget.

The 'new' Poor Law had been introduced in 1834 and that law meant the poor had a choice; work and survive or seek help by going to a workhouse. There was no in-between. The new law was an act passed to amend previous poor laws to limit the cost of relief to the poor and prevent anyone other than the utterly poverty-stricken and impecunious from applying for help. And even if you were desperate enough to seek help at the workhouse, the conditions there were not something you'd wish to endure. One of the workhouses in Southampton was situated in St Mary's Street and by 1843 it was terribly oversubscribed: 'overcrowded with four to a bed and no segregation of the sexes'. To add to this the drainage, ventilation and supplies of water were 'totally inadequate'. The workhouse at St Mary's Street meant that many desperate people had to be turned away because it's 220 inmate capacity meant it could 'hold only one fifth of the town's paupers.'[6]

The workhouse was still an absolute necessity for some of the city's poor even in 1912. But if you became a 'workhouse child', the name stuck. Children who had to live there were dressed in the workhouse clothing and were often singled out by non-workhouse children, as was recorded in a letter to the local paper the *Southern Daily Echo* in September 1977 when a reader wrote:

> 'As I was born in Chapel 75 years ago, I remember the workhouse very well. [There was] a large house where the children were kept. They used to be taken to and from Ascupant school by an attendant. They used to wear a workhouse uniform so everyone knew them and used to call them "the workhouse kids".'

Ways to earn your keep in the workhouse consisted of agricultural work or chopping wood for male workers, needlework and washing for female adults, more agricultural labour or tailoring for boys and needlework and washing for girls.

Thankfully there are no records of William or Emily needing to seek help from the workhouse. William, so my aunt Doreen tells me, was in work 'as much as he could possibly be'. A hard-working man, keeping a wage coming in must have always been at the forefront of his mind. So, with sudden vacancies for crew, on 6 April 1912 William left Emily and the five children at his home on Henry Road, walked down to Canute Road to the White Star Line office and signed on to the *Titanic*. His job would be as a fireman and he would earn monthly wages of £6 – equivalent to around £469 at the time of writing this book. Men all over the city were doing the same. Some were single, hoping for adventure and to see New York. Others were new grooms, the wedding flowers still fresh, sailing off to earn enough to set up home when they returned. Others, like William, were older husbands and fathers desperate to be able to pay one more month's rent and feed their children. As a painful symbol of how poor many of these men were, pawn shops displayed these men's best shoes in their windows. With no gold or rings, male crew members instead pawned their shoes in exchange for money to leave their wives while they were away. There are no references of my great-grandfather pawning his shoes. Maybe he had no best shoes to pawn. Or maybe, as they lived in the suburbs of the city, rather than the much poorer areas closer to the docks, he and Emily were not so destitute that it was necessary. Still, the excitement in the house on Henry Road when it was confirmed William would have work on the RMS *Titanic* must have been contagious. Although, to sign on as a fireman was not something to be hugely proud of; it was not as esteemed a job as, say, an engineer or steward in the higher decks. In fact, a cousin I found while researching this book told me that William was called an 'engineer', even by his own family, because of the negative associations of being part of the Black Gang who were known for their heavy drinking and fights.[7] But being a Black Gang member required a certain level of fitness and ability, as investigated in the evocative book *Down Amongst the Black Gang* by Richard P. de Kerbrech; the main attributes being 'fitness, strength, stamina and endurance and also a high tolerance for heat was mandatory as the temperatures in the stokehold sometimes reached 120F. They needed the intelligence to pace themselves and the ability to work as a team.'[8] Yet, despite having to display these characteristics to get their work, the stokers were seen as the lowest of the low and 'were treated as if they were uneducated lower-class labourers, an attitude born of the tremendous class distinction of the period.'

Whatever your job, the chance to work on *the* vessel of the age would have been an incredible one. And for working class passengers, too, the trip would have been life-changing. Many of the any third-class steerage passengers had bought their ticket on *Titanic* as a passage to a new life in America. The hope pulsating through the city, both from crew and working-class passengers dreaming of a new life across the Atlantic, would have been tangible. Did Emily hug William with excitement when he came home and told her he'd been accepted as a fireman? Did she gather the five children around the kitchen table to celebrate their father's success? Perhaps she pointed out those yellow funnels down at the docks, visible from so many streets around the city, to her little ones, explaining that Father would be sailing on the ship that all the newspapers were talking about. A city like Southampton would have had hundreds of men in every area and street who worked in some way connected with the docks and the ships that sailed from them. Emily likely would have had neighbours whose husbands had also found work on *Titanic*. I imagine her running to a friend in a nearby street to tell the news; her William was going to work on the greatest ship of the age, and they'd be able to pay the rent and eat reasonably for a few weeks.

Amidst such poverty, it's almost easy to forget that women were fighting for the suffrage movement at the same time, with reports of vocal women in the local newspapers in 1911 imploring listeners to consider women's right to vote. 'Think then of the women working in the mills and in the shops: are they to have no voice in the making of the laws which limit and govern their work? Think of the wives and mothers throughout the country: is it right to legislate for the homes or the children without giving them their say?' wrote one woman in a letter to the *Southampton Times and Hampshire Express* in 1912. But suffragettes were beginning to become tired of imploring people to listen. The local papers of the time now began to include news stories of suffragettes appearing in court for breaking windows and other public order offences. Their cause was a noble one, but one that would take years in coming for the likes of my great-grandmother. Working class women like Emily and many other wives of seafaring men were too busy fighting to survive to fight for their right to vote. Most references to women in the newspapers of the time are adverts for corsets and treatments for chapped hands from washing. Other regular advertisements were for Dr Williams' Pink Pills for women 'held in the clutch of anaemia' and who 'live robbed of their strength and brightness…their steps languid and every attitude tells of an unhappy existence.'

But a storm was brewing. Women were sick of being tired and languid. The same year the mighty and, arguably, very *male Titanic* was to sail, was the same year the women's suffrage movement reached an enormous turning point; a climax. For years the National Union of Women's Suffrage Societies (NUWSS), the suffragists, and Women's Social and Political Union (WSPU), the suffragettes, had been campaigning for more awareness for the rights of women. But in 1912, things became more militant. While president of the NUWSS Millicent Fawcett still campaigned in her middle-class peaceful way, the suffragettes wanted action faster. The famous saying of suffragette leader Emmeline Pankhurst was 'deeds, not words' and so suffragettes began smashing windows, setting fire to public property, chaining themselves to railings and going on hunger strike when arrested. Public outcry at their behaviour was so great that the National League for Opposing Women's Suffrage was founded in 1910, two years before RMS *Titanic* would set sail. The League released the notorious poster advert featuring a hard-working man returning home after another day's slog to find his house in chaos, detritus everywhere, the children sobbing on the table and the floor, because the absent mother has gone to a suffragette meeting. This was the paradoxical, seismic world in which my great-grandmother Emily was living and rearing children. On the one hand, it was the era which launched the *Titanic* representing everything masculine, technological and powerful of the age. On the other hand, it was the era of the struggle of very real women like her and their desperate fight to be heard, recognized and counted. But dreams of the opportunity to have a say in the nation's politics were a long way off for someone like her. Poverty and child-rearing have a way of making a person focus on the here and now, not the future. Her day would have been filled with staying alive; feeding her five children, doing the backbreaking work of laundry in a copper bath-tub, day in, day out. If shoes had holes in their soles, they remained that way. Even if William did come into work at the docks, Emily would have known it wouldn't last long. Seafaring men in Southampton were casually employed. As 'MG' says, 'Yes there was hardship right through all those days an' if you, if you, if you 'ad a job in those days you were lucky.'

It wasn't just a case of the roulette game that was finding work and losing work at the docks, either. Working as a seafaring man or labourer at the docks was dangerous – sometimes before you even set sail. Tales abounded of men killed or maimed in accidents on ships or at the docks. One such case, published in the local paper, had the rather descriptive headline: 'Whirled round a winch.' The story was about Ernest Harland, aged 19. His 'body [was] all tangled up in the wire rope round the barrel of the winch.'[9] The man died. The news report included the fact that his would-be rescuer was also knocked unconscious. So, even if you found work and even if you weren't even at sea, the ships and docks were still physically-demanding, dangerous places to be.

The great transatlantic liners of the day were also not immune to accident and tragedy. In 1901, the White Star Line ship RMS *Oceanic*, which my great-grandfather worked on as a fireman, collided with the SS *Kincora*. Seven people were killed. Four years later, *Oceanic* was the first ever White Star Line ship to suffer a mutiny of angry stokers, furious at their working conditions. Thirty-five firemen were convicted and jailed. And even *Titanic*'s sister ship, the White Star Line's *Olympic*, had a collision on her fifth voyage in September 1911. She was sailing parallel to the British ship HMS *Hawke* when she turned starboard and HMS *Hawke* was unable to avoid her in time. The bow of HMS *Hawke* collided with the starboard side of RMS *Olympic* which tore two holes in her hull, meaning that the previously watertight compartments filled with water. *Olympic* had to return to Southampton port. There were no fatalities or injuries, but it was a sign that even the great advanced liners of the modern age were not invincible. It was also a dark portent of what would become of her sister ship RMS *Titanic* a year later, albeit on a catastrophically fatal scale.

Yet, the great ocean liner age with all its glamour, eminent passengers, luxury and decadence was evolving, growing and becoming ever more opulent and, simply, *big*. Size mattered. RMS *Oceanic*, was, until *Titanic* came along, the largest ship in the world. But the White Star Line were touting their ships RMS *Adriatic, Olympic, Oceanic* and, of course, *Titanic* as their 'big four'. When *Titanic* was announced as the largest vessel of them all at just over 52,000 tonnes, the world waited in awe to see this enormous creation that would carry everyone from the wealthiest aristocrats to the poorest steerage passengers to a life in the New World. Her launch from Belfast a year earlier was reported in a local newspaper describing how there was a 'roar of cheering from the workmen on the decks. The men below took up the cheering and the mighty ship passed down the well-greased ways.'

Workmen might well have cheered. The age of luxury long-distance travel by ship was entering a new dawn and *Titanic* would be queen. Her interior was unparalleled, with its neoclassical style grand staircase made from English oak as well as all the mod cons of the age including Turkish baths, a swimming pool, a gym and a lounge modelled after the Palace of Versailles. She wasn't simply a breathtakingly beautiful ship, she was a state of mind; a physical manifestation of the power and grandeur held by a lucky few to enjoy. Compare if you will, the dank, mould-ridden two-up, two-down hovels where many of the lower members of the *Titanic*'s crew lived with the decadent cabins in first class. The suites were decorated in lavish styles and had every modern electrical gadget going, such as telephones, bells to call stewards, heaters to warm them and fans to cool them. Many larger suites had interconnecting rooms so that children might sleep in one part of the cabin and the husband and wife in another and, of course, the staff in another area. Second class cabins, although nowhere near as lavish, were comfortable and included bunk-bed style berths, a basin and chamber pot in case you couldn't make it to the communal bathroom. Third class were similar to second but smaller and housed up to ten passengers. A first-class ticket began at £30, around £2,820 today. But even a third-class passage cost £7, a lot by today's standards at £659.

Of course, lowly members of the Black Gang such as my great-grandfather would not have had a hope of touching the ornate oak banister of the grand staircase or lifting a weight in the exclusive gym. He would never have even seen a deck higher than his own and the boiler rooms. But other members of the crew could indeed witness the ship's splendour. Many men – and some women – joined the crew of the *Titanic* as stewards in first, second and third class. They worked in the dining rooms, public lounges and the gym and swimming pools and on-deck as well as in the passengers' cabins serving food, changing linen and providing towels and toiletries. One such steward from Southampton was Alfred Henry Whitford who had been born on the island of Guernsey but had married a local Southampton girl, Louisa Ellen Browning, in 1906. He was a second-class steward and would receive monthly wages of £3 15 shillings. The couple lived in Richmond Street, Southampton and next door to them another steward had set sail called John Brookman who had married his fiancée, Alice Roberts, the Sunday before he'd set sail. Had he eagerly accepted his £3 monthly wages as a third-class steward in the knowledge that the money would go towards setting up home with Alice when he returned? Perhaps they'd talked of having children. There was great pride in getting a job on the world's most beautiful and largest ship, especially as a steward who would wear a smart uniform. As a new groom, John Brookman must have felt on top of the world, knowing what he earned in wages – and tips, if he got them – would all go towards the start of married life with Alice. There are tales in the archives and newspapers and collated by *Titanic* experts all over of these men's hopes and dreams. In many of the films, however, these workers are no more than background characters, extras. Just as they were invisible to the rich, so are they to us as viewers. But they too had their dreams, as did their wives and sweethearts waving them off from the shore. Many were saving their pay to carry on or start new lives back home on their return. Some were newlyweds who'd only just said their vows, others had sweethearts they hoped to propose to when they came home. Mothers, too, often relied on the income of their seafaring sons. One mother, Mrs Burrows, had a son named Harry who had waited to get the chance to sign on. In an interview given in the *Southampton Times and Hampshire Express*, she later said, 'My son Harry goes to sea and he stayed home for a month in the expectation of getting engaged on the *Titanic*.' But for some fortuitous reason at the last minute, Harry changed his mind and didn't go.

But, of course, just like life today in any city or town, not all these relationships were happy, loving, or even simple. One notorious example is that of William Mintram, aged 46 in 1912, who signed on as a fireman, like my great-grandfather. They would have been colleagues and perhaps known each other. William Mintram was married, but very unhappily so. Ten years before the *Titanic* sailed, William had come home to his house in Chapel Road, Southampton and rowed with his wife because she had pawned his son's boots to pay for drink. Police had reported hearing the furore as they rowed. During the argument, William Mintram then stabbed his wife in the back, killing her. He was charged with murder but in his defence, he explained that his wife had attacked him first, he was drunk, and the rest was a blank. Incredibly, he was found guilty only of manslaughter and was sentenced to 12 years' penal servitude. He was released three years later, possibly because he had children to provide for. A decade later and a free man, William Mintram signed on to *Titanic*. Did the White Star Line care if they hired convicted criminals? For the boiler rooms and the notorious Black Gang, unseen by the passenger and known as hard-working, hard-drinking men, perhaps not. But for Mintram, like many others, this opportunity to join *Titanic* would have been a new start, a chance to start afresh.

In fact, that sense of new beginnings, of hope, of a more positive future pumped through the city's heart after a long time of dark despair during the coal strike. *Titanic*'s arrival and departure on her maiden voyage from Southampton would have generated money for the city's businesses and the local economy, too. Local firms provided everything for the *Titanic*'s voyage from sausages to cut flowers and plants, from beer to fruit and vegetables. Even uniforms were tailored at one of the city's firms, Miller's Naval Tailors.[10] The sheer range of jobs made available on the ship were varied from officers, able seamen, stewards, chefs, deck crew, engineers, a plumber, restaurant staff, postal clerks, musicians, firemen, greasers and trimmers. Of course, it was not only men who made up the crew of *Titanic*, although they did make up the lion's share. Of the 913 crew, there are 23 female crew members recorded who worked as stewardesses, cashiers and one as a matron. Twelve of these female crew members were married. One of them was Kate Gold who had married John Hannah Gold in Salford, Lancashire twenty years before *Titanic* sailed. But the marriage had not worked out and she had gone on to work on ships such as RMS *Adriatic* as a stewardess, then on the RMS *Olympic*. She had no children and signed on to *Titanic*, again as a stewardess. A fellow stewardess was Annie Martha Martin, who had separated from her husband. And then there were the young members of crew. Two 14-year-old boys signed on as crew. Frederick William Hopkins signed on as a plates steward and William Albert Watson as a bellboy. By today's standards, many parents would have been sick with worry at such young boys going to sea to work. The idea seems unthinkable. But in 1912, many if not most working-class boys of that age would have been employed in some form. Apprentices often began working at age 12 to bring money into the family home. Emily's eldest son Charles, who was 15 when *Titanic* sailed, worked as an errand boy, bringing his wages into the family pot to add to that of this father William's. So these two 14-year-olds onboard *Titanic*, although by our standards children, were considered very much 'men.'

After leaving Belfast on 2 April 1912, *Titanic* steamed in to Southampton, docked and brought with her the scent of hope and an economic boom for the future. In a city emerging from a coal strike, hope would have been something you could almost taste on the air whether you were the highest-ranking officer or a scullion. Newspapers of the time were brimming with stories of the famous names who would be sailing on the maiden voyage in first class, from businessmen John Jacob Astor and Benjamin Guggenheim to Isador and Ida Strauss, co-owners of Macy's department store. For these international big names to be stepping from Southampton's docks onto *Titanic* would have been like the world's biggest modern-day movie stars arriving in a provincial city today. The local papers and nationals alike reported in flurries. For a few days, Southampton was the focus of the whole world. When the great ship was opened for the paying public in Southampton for a preview on 5 April 1912, there were news reports that the 'privileged few who have had the pleasure of visiting the ship since her arrival at Southampton on Thursday morning have been at a loss to express their admiration.'[11] She was, stated journalists, simply the most breathtakingly beautiful ship ever designed.

Men, women, children, mothers, fathers, sons, daughters, all stood at Southampton docks to wave off *Titanic* on her maiden voyage on 10 April 1912. My father told me that his mother said Emily was amongst that crowd of tens of thousands people with her five children. Perhaps the younger ones waved hankies in the air, hoping innocently their father William might see their faces in the crowd. But he would have already been at work, deep in the bowels of the ship, stoking the furnaces to power the mighty vessel as she set sail. As *Titanic* was towed out by tug boats, though, disaster very nearly struck. As she began to sail away from her position in dock next to the ship the SS *New York*, she caused the other ship to break away from where she was docked next to another liner the *Oceanic*. The result was that the *Titanic* and *New York* narrowly missed hitting each other, causing 'considerable consternation among the hundreds of people who had gathered on the quayside to witness the sailing of the largest vessel afloat.'[12]

It was only a near miss. *New York* was tugged back into position and all was well. But was this near-miss that delayed the *Titanic's* departure by one hour a strange omen of what was to come? If it was, the happy crowd didn't feel anything was amiss. As the tens of thousands who waved her off smiled and called out good wishes to those onboard, they could never have imagined what would happen to her just five days later. They would never have dreamed that the ship of dreams, the 'unsinkable', opulent, decadent symbol of the age would be no more, and over 1,500 people dead.

As Emily and her children waved off the ship, jostling and craning their necks to see over the mass of raised arms, hankies and hats aloft, the world must have seemed so very hopeful, so joyful, and on the brink of new prosperous times to come.

Chapter 2

Wives and Sweethearts,
Stewards and Sailors

As *Titanic* set off down the Solent en route to her first stop at Cherbourg, flags and caps on shore were still waving furiously. Gradually, though, the excitable crowds dispersed, carrying on the party atmosphere as people made their way home. Emily would have made her way back to her house two miles away in Henry Road and got on with the normal daily chores, as did the crew's other family members all over town. This is the point at which most *Titanic* books and film representations of those working-class hat-and-hankie-waving family members end. These family members vanish, to be eclipsed by the tragedy of the lives lost onboard, or the sheer opulence of the ship itself. In films, the stewards, firemen and restaurant staff disperse and become fuzzy, faceless figures while the rich and aristocratic take centre stage. But who were the *Titanic* crew and their womenfolk? Where did they live and what were the women's lives like, relying on seafaring men at a time of great economic uncertainty?

Just as *Titanic* was divided into layers of class from the first-class crème de la crème on the top decks down to the firemen such as my great-grandfather at the very bottom in the boiler rooms, so were the crew's womenfolk. The top crew member himself, Captain Edward Smith, had married Sarah Eleanor Pennington in Winwick, Lancashire in 1887. When Captain Smith set sail on RMS *Titanic,* he was 62 and Sarah was 51. They had a daughter, Helen, who was 14 when *Titanic* left Southampton. They lived in a large house in a leafy part of the city and were comfortably-off. Captain Smith was the highest-paid sea captain of the time and his monthly earnings were just over £100 – a great deal more than my great-grandfather on his £6 a month. Smith had joined White Star Line in 1880 and had worked his way up from fourth officer on the ship SS *Celtic* to Captain of RMS *Baltic*, RMS *Adriatic*, RMS *Olympic*, and, in 1912, RMS *Titanic*. Smith became so internationally well-respected that the millionaire passengers and socialites of the day would specifically seek out ships where he was captain, as they felt in safe hands with him in control. The house where Captain Smith's wife and daughter lived was in Winn Road, Highfield, Southampton. Sadly, the large house no longer exists and is now replaced with a block of flats but it's clear that the Smith's home would have been in a very comfortable area, far away from the bustle of the docks and the poverty that many of his crew lived in day by day.

A couple of miles away in Henry Road, life for my great-grandmother Emily would have been very different from that of the captain's wife. Emily was born Emily Ellen Cull in 1874 to parents Alexander and Sarah Cull, rural-dwelling farm labourers, and she had nine siblings. She married William, my great-grandfather, who was listed as a labourer on their wedding certificate when she was 19. They said their vows on Christmas Day (the only day agricultural labourers could get a day off) in December 1893 at St Matthew's Church, Netley Marsh, which was then the rural surrounds of Southampton. William was the son of farm labourers who appeared not to have married. Did this bother Emily? Perhaps, at first. But not enough to stop her marrying him. Did he charm her with his thick-set build and his (in my opinion) rather dashing moustache? On their wedding certificate, Emily's occupation is a blank space with a black line through it. So at that point, she didn't work. Most working-class unmarried women had to, though, with many in domestic service or working in the booming textile factories. After their wedding, Emily set up home with William, moving from their farming, country roots to central Southampton. Four years after their wedding, their first son Charles Bessant was born. A daughter, Gladys, followed, then it appears another child died in infancy. My grandmother, Florence Maude, followed, then two more sons Leonard and Albert. Large families were, of course, completely normal in those days. With no real contraception barring coitus interruptus, wives spent a great deal of their lives pregnant or raising their children. As my aunt told me, 'My mother wondered if Emily and William would have ever stopped having babies'. Make of that what you will but I, ever the romantic, like to think it meant they were very happy and in love. But I'm under no illusion that love took a back seat to surviving for working class families in the early part of the twentieth century. However, my great-grandparents, it seems, lived in a slightly more comfortable area of the city where you would more likely find stewards for *Titanic* rather than burly, rough members of the Black Gang. A couple of miles east, by the docks, were the seafaring areas proper – Chapel and Northam. This was the true docklands community, the place where most seafaring men were born and bred. Most of the stokers, greasers and trimmers for *Titanic* came from these areas. Seeing men return from their jobs on other large ships of the age was a normal occurrence in the docklands areas, as was recorded in an interview for *Chapel and Northam: An Oral History of Southampton's Dockland Communities 1900-1945*:

> 'All the people around Chapel, it was a rough fighting area because they used to come home from their voyages which were "killer ships": they all came home like walking skeletons, the stokers, and they had one glorious booze up which led to fighting and then off they went again.'[1]

I've asked my aunt if anyone in the family remembered tales of my great-grandfather William joining his stoker, 'skeleton' mates for glorious drink-fuelled fights but have drawn a blank. But he would have had to be tough, hard and to take no nonsense. But, just as stories of my family have been passed down the generations, the same has happened in many other families in Southampton. During my research for this book, I discovered many descendants of *Titanic*'s crew still living in the area, each with their own fascinating family history about their ancestors. One such relative told me about his great-great uncle, Alfred Henry Self. Tony Cove, Alfred Self's great-great nephew told me that Alfred was born in Southampton in 1872 and married Caroline Calloway in 1894. A year later, Caroline gave birth to a son, Albert. Like my great-grandfather, Alfred Self worked as a stoker on steam ships. According to Tony Cove, the Selfs' son Albert was then listed at another address as a 'nurse child' and then subsequently as an adopted child. Other records of the family in relation to *Titanic* list them as childless. So, what happened? Were they unable to afford to care for their son? Did Alfred go to sea to earn more to support their child? It may well have been the case, because poverty was everywhere. Ships were a source of work, but also a source of escape. One Southampton resident from that era recalled how his father suddenly left the family for a new life in Australia without even telling his wife. The man recalled how his mother was:

> 'left with four children and she was carrying me. She was pregnant with me and …there was nothing for it, in those days, we 'ad to go the work'ouse. That was the only place. There was no social security or anything. To the work'ouse an' that's where we went, an' that's where we grew up.'[2]

The workhouse would have been a truly last resort, a place no one wanted to end up. With life hard, grim, meagre and, at times, hopeless, it seems fair to say that the *Titanic* crew's womenfolk had to be as tough and steely as the burliest stoker husband. Women may not have earned the money, but they certainly toiled behind closed doors. In an age before the luxuries we now take for granted, washing, cooking and keeping house would have taken up most of the day, every day. One interviewee who lived at the time recalled how his mother used to do the family's washing on an old scrubbing board which was no more than a plank of wood:

> 'By her feet she had piles of washing. She used to have a copper stick with clothes on it out of the copper that was bubbling away and she used to bring it right across to the bath. It must have burnt her hands. She put the copper lid back on to keep the water hot and the fire going. She used to scrub away and she had bowls all over the place, enamel bowls…I have seen mum's fingers rubbed absolutely raw with washing Dad's stuff.'[3]

My great-grandmother's daily life would have been similar – washing, cleaning, preparing food. But she had her eldest son Charlie, then a teenager of working age, to bring money into the house too. Perhaps that is how they could afford to live in a different area of the city to where many of the stokers and coal trimmers lived. At the time his father William had set sail on *Titanic*, Charlie was listed in a census as an errand boy, so Emily's housekeeping money would have been augmented by his earnings. But other women were not so fortunate.

One such woman was Lucy Violet Snape. Lucy had married Lawrence Snape, a seaman, in 1909 and they then had a daughter, Margaret Isabel. His work on ships meant they moved around a great deal and even moved as a family to Singapore. But tragedy struck. Lawrence developed dysentery while abroad and then died in China. Lucy was left a widow with a one-year-old daughter. She returned to Britain and lived with her parents. Her father then managed to pull strings to get Lucy a job as a second-class stewardess on a rather famous new ship; *Titanic*. It would be her first ever job and she had to make the heart-wrenching decision to leave her baby behind with her parents so she could earn money to support them both. She was 22 when she signed on to the *Titanic* and set sail. For a mother to leave such a young baby behind to go to work must have been very hard, particularly a woman who would have until then relied solely on her husband's earnings. It shows the desperation of many of the crew – male or female – who took jobs on the *Titanic*.

But life wasn't only dark and hopeless. There are fond memories of the folk who lived in these seafaring communities too. One interviewee who lived in Chapel said that one of the positives of being so poor was that no one ever had to lock their doors there because there was nothing to steal.[4] Well-known local midwives went door to door helping Chapel and Northam women give birth and then tended to them for days afterwards. Children were as close-knit as their parents were with their neighbours. Woe-betide if children from another area ventured into the streets or they'd be set upon by the Northam and Chapel kids in what one interviewee who lived there referred to as fondly as 'good old-fashioned, friendly fighting.'[5] With most of the men working in similar seafaring jobs, the women left behind would have been close friends, helping each other, supporting each other, lending each other money or food in times of need and an ear over the garden fence when times got tough. But as wholesome and rose-tinted as this now seems, the poverty was unrelenting. Many children were too poor to even have shoes to get to school and parents would often pawn children's school shoes or uniforms on Friday for the weekend, only to get the clothing back for Monday morning again. Many of these children did not eat all day as school meals had to be paid for and they had to spend the day trying to learn and concentrate while their hunger burned. School itself, in any case, must have felt a futile exercise to many of the children, seeing as most of the boys would be expected to follow in their fathers' footsteps on the big ships and the girls had little hope at all of anything more than marriage and babies.

It wasn't only wives and children who relied on their father's seafaring income. Many mothers relied on their sons' earnings as they went to sea and these sons would have been encouraged to follow their fathers into finding work on ships. It was a boy's assumed destiny. Percival Albert Blake was one such son who signed on to *Titanic* as a coal trimmer who may have worked alongside my great-grandfather or certainly known him. I found his descendant through social media and discovered that he lived with his parents Edwin and Clara Blake in the Chapel area along with his sister Millie. Edwin was working as a labourer at the docks, so perhaps Percival followed his father into the trade. Wifeless and childless, Percival would have gone to work on *Titanic* to bring back his earnings into the home where the whole family, including pregnant sister Millie, who was still working in a laundry, were living under one roof. If boys were too young to go to sea like their fathers, they often became errand boys or, more famously, one of the Gordon Boys, the eponymous group so named in memory of General Gordon who had once lived in Southampton. Gordon Boys carried messages and did other menial work, as one interviewee recounted in an oral history project in Southampton Archives:

> 'When I left school at 14, it was the only thing I could get with some other boys... Other kids from Chapel, Northam and Shirley. Quite a lot of big houses, or shops, might send for a Gordon Boy and the pay was sixpence for an hour's work, from which the brigade took two pence of it.'[6]

Life was a struggle. Children were not children very long before they too had to worry about money and making ends meet. But hardship has a way of bonding people together like no other and life in the docklands communities and other streets of Southampton that housed sea-faring families. was based on firm friendships and, simply, helping each other out. In the wonderfully evocative oral history book *Chapel and*

Northam edited by Sheila Jemima, one interviewee recalled how everyone shared what they did have with those who had not:

> 'Community life although it was hard, there was never anything better for people being as one, because I remember in the street I lived in, one of the ladies there across the road, her husband had a pretty good job with Union Castle Line and so they were able to buy a bungalow bath, they were the only ones in the street that had a bungalow bath…and when her husband went off back to sea that bath went up and down the street, everybody borrowing it to have a bath.'

There was tremendous camaraderie and sisterhood among sailors' wives, too. Women might not have been able to afford a doctor or even a midwife if times were hard. But when a woman had a baby, the female neighbours knew she'd need support. They rallied round, one cleaning, another cooking, someone else taking on the washing to add to their own endless pile. They'd even cook the new mother's husband's dinner while she recovered in bed.

Many residents recalled colourful characters too, such as the muffin man, musicians, rare times the circus came to town and a well-loved Italian community who ran ice-cream shops frequented by the locals. Life was a colourful mix of gruff seamen returning home from the ships, hard, stoical wives and all the relationships and friendships that intertwined. But in life, these people were never far from death with diphtheria being rife, as recorded in the Northam Girls' School log in 1906 that one of the girls had been taken into isolation with the disease and that there appeared to be 'much sickness about the parish.'

My aunt recalls her mother remembering being taken ill with the 'flu and being sent to bed for days with her sister Gladys. Doctors were a luxury few could afford and so many children became ill or even died of illnesses we consider all but eradicated in Britain today. Damp, cold living conditions made these diseases more prevalent amongst the poor. This wasn't helped by the severe flooding that happened in the dockland residential areas regularly during high tide. Entire ground floors of houses were submerged and furniture and belongings ruined. It is testament to these people's hardiness and good humour that they were able to live not only on such meagre, irregular earnings but also while spending a lot of their time battling illness such as consumption and diphtheria and bailing out water from their homes.

As for my great-grandmother Emily, she was a hardy sort too, with five children to look after and William often away at sea. She'd had to adapt from an agricultural life to that of a bustling maritime city with her husband absent most of the time on the boats. My aunt told me that my grandmother recalled a very happy childhood in their rented home in the Freemantle area of Southampton and that they were 'not ashamed' of the street or the house where they lived. Perhaps this was because the Freemantle and Shirley areas which were further away from the docklands housing were, arguably, slightly more comfortable places to live and certainly not at risk from the regular flooding the residents of Chapel and Northam so often had to endure. Houses here were generally small and terraced with no gas or electricity and water only to be found in the back garden.[7] In Freemantle, accounts from the day recall there was a hotel, a sweet shop and general store, a fishmonger, greengrocer, barber shop and furniture shop. The street also had a laundry, a shoe repair shop, a corn chandler and pubs. This area was certainly more suburb than city proper. Horse and carts would deliver milk and pass on the streets and the residents would rush out into the road with their shovels to take the manure.[8]

Many of the stewards who signed up for *Titanic* listed Shirley or Freemantle streets as their addresses. There was Edward Bessant – no relation to my great-grandfather – who signed on as a baggage steward and lived in a road not far from my great-grandparents. Fifteen minutes' walk away from my ancestors' house lived 38-year-old Edward Martin Hendy, who signed on as a first-class steward. He had a wife, Alice, and lived next door to his brother Albert, who also signed on as a steward. And a few streets away in Elgin Road, William Ford Kingscote lived with his wife Mary and their four children. He signed on as a first-class steward and would receive £3 15s. Mary must have been thrilled that her husband would be working near to the crème de la crème of international society, but perhaps far more thrilled with his earnings that would surely go towards supporting their four children. There are many more tales of stewards from this area of the city – the streets must have buzzed with talk of which class they'd be serving and what they'd experience on board. If the docklands area was for firemen and trimmers, the area where my great-grandparents lived was well and truly stewards' central with almost every street having a man signing on to *Titanic*. And one road in particular was truly its hub – Malmesbury Road. Here, eight men found jobs on the ship: John Downing Smillie, 25, a first class saloon steward; Albert White (who signed on as R. Morrell), 21, a trimmer; Edwin Best, 40, a first class steward and married to Annie Elizabeth Pike; Edward Alfred Orlando Stroud, 19, a second class steward; Alfred Allsop, 34, electrician and married to Hilda; Herbert George Hensford, 26, assistant butcher; William James Revell, 31, a first class steward and married to Blanche; and James Addison Toshack, 31, a first class saloon steward. James was married to Phoebe and was originally from Scotland. You can imagine the excitement and chatter on this street, not only between the men who were near neighbours who knew each other but from their wives and families too. The incomes of eight families were about to be augmented by their men getting jobs on *Titanic*. Talk must have been of nothing else in Malmesbury Road. Here was a street that had won the jackpot.

One Southampton man who signed on as a greaser was Frederick Woodford. On 11 April, after picking up passengers in Cherbourg, *Titanic* docked at Queenstown, Ireland. From there, Frederick Woodford sent his wife Susan a letter. In it, Frederick, who was father to two daughters, told Susan where to go to collect his pay from the White Star Line in Southampton. It seems early on in the journey to write to a wife. Did he write to her so soon after *Titanic* had set sail because he'd learned exactly where she should go to collect his pay? Or did he write to her because he was already missing her and thinking about her and his two daughters back at home?

From another part of Southampton, Harry Yearsley, then 38, signed on as a saloon steward. Harry was married to Flora and they had five children. My social media searches led me to Harry Yearsley's great-grandson who sent me a photograph of Harry looking incredibly dapper on deck of a ship, smiling at the camera, pipe jauntily in his mouth. Other relatives came forward too. Lorraine Keys told me of her ancestor William Thomas Kerley, who had signed on to *Titanic* as an assistant second class saloon steward and lived with his parents at the time. Kerley was 28 when he boarded and he died in the sinking. But his body was recovered, and along with it some of his personal effects. These were shared with me by Lorraine. A wallet, a photograph and a letter were found on his body. It appeared he had plans; he was courting a young woman who was working in service because the letter found on him was from his sweetheart named 'Let'. In her letter, which Lorraine kindly let me have a transcript of, 'Let' writes:

> 'My Dearest Tom, Many thanks for your nice letter which I received on Monday the day you left … well dear have you settled when you are to start on your first sea voyage. I do hope dear that you will take great care of yourself and have our weather, it will not be so bad when you are more used to the sea…will close with fondest love from your loving Let.'

Kerley never came home to start a life with Let.

Another descendant I traced on social media told me of his great-grandfather John Edward Puzey, who signed on as a first-class steward. Mike Knowlton was kind enough to meet me and told me that John had a wife, Rose, and two sons. In the photograph Mike Knowlton shared with me, taken before the disaster, John Puzey stands as a proud man, his wife sitting beside him with their two boys. John stands looking out of shot while the rest of the family look at the camera. John Puzey died in the sinking aged 44. I met with Mike Knowlton and we pondered as to whether John's expression, looking off into the distance, could be described as eerily seeing his own future. Photographs were not cheap in those days and to no doubt after the tragedy, Rose Puzey would have treasured that image of her husband staring proudly off camera.

Once descendants came forward, other stories emerged too. There was the case of father and son, both named Arthur William May. Arthur senior was married to Ann and together they had nine children. Arthur junior had spent some time living in a boarding house while his father was at sea. Both men signed on to *Titanic* in the engineering department – Arthur junior as a fireman and Arthur senior as a stokers' messman. Presumably Ann would have encouraged her son to follow his father's footsteps into a life at sea, as so many other mothers did around the city.

Lists abound of the crew and their stories, painstakingly put together by relatives, historians, academics and *Titanic* fans alike. Of course, not all were Southampton born and bred. One street where 26 crew members came from was Oxford Street because it was the address of the Sailors' Home. Many men not actually resident in the city used the Sailors' Home as their address before signing. They travelled to the city from London, Liverpool, Belfast and even the Netherlands, dumped their kit bags in a room and slept there until they boarded their boat. Single or married, fathers or not yet fathers, these men all signed on in the hope of a successful voyage earning money for their families in Southampton or elsewhere.

On 13 April 1912, *Titanic* sailed through calm seas. While the stokers, greasers and trimmers toiled in the boiler rooms, while the stewards ensured doors were opened for passing aristocrats and notables, that glass was clean, beverages were served and bedding in the rooms was primped and perfect, the wealthy dined and drank in first class without a care in the world. *Titanic* was one glorious dream of fine dining, of the finest wines and champagnes, the very best leisure facilities. Women promenaded on deck while their husbands enjoyed cigarettes in the smoking lounges. Some enjoyed some exercise in the exclusive gym. While my great-grandmother would have cooked dinner and cleaned up back at home, William would have been on his four-hours-on, eight-hours-off shift pattern in the sweltering boiler room. On 14 April, as *Titanic* sailed through the North Atlantic Ocean, seven iceberg warnings were received via wireless from nearby ships. *Titanic* was sailing into dangerous waters. But nothing was done to change course. This great ship, after all, was unsinkable. On the evening of the 14 April, the ship's notables dined on rich food and chatted late into the night. Perhaps they felt strange vibrations beneath them, but it was explained away that the captain had plans to reach New York early to make the papers and dazzle the world all over again. At 11.40 pm, the lookout Frederick Fleet stared out from the crows' nest and into the freezing darkness. He didn't have a pair of binoculars. But he suddenly saw something terrible straight ahead. *Iceberg.* He rang the bell and called the bridge and yelled, 'Iceberg! Right ahead!' Up at the wheel, quartermaster Robert Hichens was steering *Titanic*. He tried to turn but it was too late. The iceberg, which newspaper reports at the time described as anything between 50 and 100 feet tall and 200 to 400 feet long, was too immense, too wide and too deep. The ship was also going at 22.5 knots, just 0.5 knots beneath the maximum speed of 23. Despite all attempts to turn, to evade it, the iceberg penetrated the starboard side of *Titanic*, searing a huge gash in her of over 220 feet.

Water began to pour in below decks as late-night diners and drinkers carried on their party in first class. Three thousand miles away, back in Southampton, the wives of the *Titanic* crew slept deeply after another day of exhausting housework. As their children dreamt perhaps of the circus visiting, or of rich delicious food, or of owning a pair of shiny, dry boots they could actually keep for school, somewhere 400 miles off the coast of Newfoundland, a terrible legend was being made. *Titanic* began to sink beneath the waves. Now, I imagine those wives and children sleeping innocently in their beds in their silent terraces and I want to turn back time and wave some kind of magic spell to let them sleep just that little bit longer; to dream just a little bit more; to put off the horrific news that would come just hours later when day broke.

But of course, day did break. Through the night aboard *Titanic*, the Marconi wireless operators had been frantically sending messages to nearby ships to come to their aid. The distress call – CQD (Come. Quick. Danger) – was sent out by Jack Phillips, the senior wireless operator. Sister ship, RMS *Olympic*, who was within 500 miles of *Titanic*, messaged back that they were on their way and began racing to help. But it would be RMS *Carpathia* who would reach the foundering vessel, some four hours after receiving distress messages. At 2.20 am local time, *Titanic* foundered.

In Southampton, meanwhile, it was past 5am. Emily got her five children up for the day. Her eldest son Charlie went off to his job as an errand boy and Emily served up breakfast. Gladys, Florence and Leonard set off for school while two-year-old Albert played on the floor. In our world of instant news, 24-hours a day; of social media messages and live-streams of happenings all over the world, it is hard to imagine that, while *Titanic* languished at the bottom of the North Atlantic, reports of the tragedy were still unconfirmed in Southampton. Then, during Monday April 15, people began to talk, to relay confusing messages from house to house and from street to street. Titanic *hit an iceberg...* Titanic *sank...Everyone aboard was saved...Many aboard are dead...*

No one in my family knows if Emily heard these rumours in her part of the city. But by a late edition of the *Southern Daily Echo* on April 15, news began to be confirmed. The first report in the *Echo* read:

'*Titanic* Collides with Iceberg in Mid-Ocean: *Olympic* and other ships to the rescue. The White Star liner *Titanic*, the world's largest and most luxurious vessel which left Southampton on Wednesday last with over 2,500 souls on board collided with an iceberg last evening in mid-Atlantic.'

Further down, in the same edition, the headline reads:

'All the passengers safe. A wireless message to Halifax states that all the passengers were safely taken off the *Titanic* at 3.30 am. The White Star Company emphasises their claim that *Titanic* is unsinkable.'

Southern Daily Echo boys would have wandered from street to street, placard in hand, shouting of *Titanic's* 'mishap' as it was initially thought to be. Perhaps Emily encountered one of these lads. Maybe she bought a paper. Perhaps a fellow crewmember's wife would have rushed to her door to tell her what had happened. Either way, as the hours passed, more news filtered slowly in and the newspapers relayed it. Pieces of information came through in infuriatingly slow and contradictory dribs and drabs, some saying that all passengers and crew were saved, others saying everyone on board had been transferred to other liners. At this stage, the feeling was still hopeful that lives on board had been saved. It appeared heroic sister ships and nearby vessels had saved everyone. *Titanic* might have hit an iceberg but it would be all right, they were told, everyone would be coming home. Even the following day, despite the *Southern Daily Echo* leading with the headline '*Titanic* Founders' and that 'all hope of salvage abandoned' there was hope. Journalists reported that many passengers and crew had been saved; that women and children had survived. There was hope that most, if not all, on board had been rescued and taken to safety.

But in subsequent reporting, that rhetoric of hope began to change. Numbers began being used instead of phrases such as 'all passengers'. A number – 675 – came up in one report in the *Southern Daily Echo*. When a reporter asked Mr James Parton, London manager of the White Star Company, if 675 meant the total amount of people saved, Mr Parton replied evasively that the Leyland liner *Californian* was staying on the spot 'in hope of picking up others'. But he also added that this was 'a dreadful disaster'. But whatever people in power were carefully saying, news was now spreading like wildfire in Southampton. With no hope of getting a wireless message, as the rich were wont to do, ordinary people began telling their neighbours what they knew, in exchange for what they might have heard. When those answers were not concrete, people began to leave their streets. They headed to Canute Road – the home of the White Star Lines offices by Southampton docks. One report, again in the local paper, detailed family members congregating outside the White Star Line offices building, where a message had finally been posted:

> '*Titanic* foundered about 2.30am April 15. About 675 crew and passengers picked up by ships boats of *Carpathia* and *California*. Remaining and searching position of disaster. Names of those saved will be posted as soon as received.'

The report then goes on to describe the emotions of those waiting, praying and hoping for news:

> 'Dismay and incredulity fought for the mastery in the faces of the anxious crowd as regulated by the police as they pressed forward to read the fateful bulletin…'

It wasn't just the White Star Line office that had a crowd forming. According to reports, nearly 95 per cent of the crew had become members of the newly formed Seafarers' Union and many family members went to the Union offices instead to ask for news. In a later reports in local papers, the sense of doom and impending horror began to be slowly confirmed, with reports of a relayed message from the ship *Carpathia* stating 'that there are 660 passengers and crew aboard and the others are drowned…' It is difficult to imagine an age without the luxury of fast-moving news; of no Twitter, Facebook or internet and no TV. News instead began to spread by word of mouth and by late newspaper editions furiously put together by journalists, adding to their reports hour by hour with extra bits of information, but always with darker and darker confirmations. More people gravitated to the docks to wait. First it was mostly men. Then more and more women came too; some carrying babies in their arms, others pushing young babies in prams. There were so many of them at one point that the queue of prams began to block the road, preventing people and traffic from passing.

If Emily slept that night, it would have been fitfully. Perhaps she didn't even try to rest. Questions would have reeled in her mind. Had more crew been saved or had they drowned? Had sister ships taken crew to safety or not? Had William made it to a lifeboat? Was he on it somewhere, out in the ocean, or had he been luckier and taken onto a large vessel and was now en route to New York and safety? Emily made the decision to walk to Canute Road with her children and try to find out the truth. But by 17 April, the mood had changed dramatically from one of disbelief mixed with hope, to one of despair and a desperate need for confirmation, however grim. 'The pathetic scenes in Southampton yesterday after the dread news that the *Titanic*'s foundering had been confirmed would have moved the hardest heart to compassion,' wrote the *Southern Daily Echo* on 17 April. The report described how firstly the crowd was mostly composed of men, then more and more women. It described how many women carried babies in their arms or had young toddlers clinging to their skirts. The report said:

> 'One heard many a sad story of loved ones aboard the ill-fated vessel, who in many cases were the breadwinners of the family and in several instances the speakers broke down and sobbed bitterly.'

Everyone reacts differently to tragedy, then or now. Some women would have sobbed. Others might have stood there in numb disbelief. It is hard for me to imagine my stern-faced ancestor Emily sobbing. Her picture taken four or five years later with her children is that of a cold, perhaps even unemotional, woman. Her eyes give nothing away, except a determination to survive and carry on. I do not know if she wept. I do not know if she broke down. I am an eternal optimist and, if that runs in my family, I imagine her more likely hoping against hope that her William would indeed be coming home. I imagine her stoically getting on with the days' chores, still sweeping up, still putting a meal together, still ticking off her children if they played up – all the while imagining that in the days to come William's name would be on a survivors' list outside the White Star Offices. She was a woman who had been hopeful and brave enough to marry an illegitimate farm hand, brave enough to leave her agricultural background for the city and to become a seaman's wife. I imagine her seizing new hope with all the fierceness she could muster. If there would be a time for crying it would be later when his death was confirmed. But not yet. While there was no news, there was still hope.

Chapter 3

Daddy Won't Be Coming Home

As the hours passed, that flicker of hope that burned in the most optimistic wives of the city began to fade away. Flags around the city flew at half-mast to honour those who were now surely dead, not missing. The bright, April light and spring sunshine seemed to mock the mere mortals standing, waiting, hoping for news outside the White Star Offices. Budding flowers, Easter and spring speak of hope to everyone – even the very poor – but there was no hope left now. Even the *Southern Daily Echo*, which had been so hopeful in the beginning, wrote of the third day of desperate family members waiting for news with a tragic tone:

> '...the shadow of death and disaster hangs over the port like
> a black thundercloud. All through the long night, a tired out
> little band of men and women kept a ceaseless vigil...'

Still, people came, they read new notices posted outside the offices of 'no news yet', before returning to their place in the crowd. Some waited hours, went away for something to eat, or to feed their children, before returning again. In any time of great tragedy, the mental and emotional journey of those who worry and long for someone's safety starts with hope, then moves on to fearing the worst, before simply longing for an answer – however terrible. No small wonder, then, that as the collective mood began to change from innocent hope to that of a despairing acceptance, that even the burliest labourers were moved: 'Women sobbed aloud while tears glistened in the eye of the rough and hardy seafaring men.'[1] These rough and hardy seafarers knew all about the risks of going to sea. Some had been involved in collisions at sea before or heard of injuries or even deaths. Sea work was hard and dangerous, exhausting and life-shortening. It shows what an enormous tragedy *Titanic* was that

32

its loss brought tears to the eyes of this kind of men. It was the greatest tragedy they had ever known.

By Wednesday 17 April, any previous positivity was ebbing away and the sense of doom and despair was tangible in the streets of Southampton. In the dockland areas of Chapel and Northam, red-eyed women talked in the street or on each other's doorsteps, begging each other for news, however small. Children were kept off school, too upset to even attempt to learn. As Northam Girls' School log recorded on April 15:

> 'A great many girls are absent this afternoon owing to the sad news regarding the 'Titanic', fathers and brothers are on the vessel and some of the little ones have been in tears all afternoon.'

Their tears would have been from grief but also from a lack of confirmation. Was their father dead or not? The uncertainty went on and on. From our twenty-first century viewpoint, when we look at old black and white photographs of children in those times with their stern little unsmiling faces and severe haircuts, they seem so distant. It seems difficult to imagine them showing such emotion at school. But these little children of history were just that; children. Like any child today who loves their father, big brother or uncle, they no doubt idolised the men in their family who went to sea, coming home with their exciting stories of foreign lands and the sense of exoticism they must have had. Emily's children would have felt the same about their father. Now they would have seen their mother's worried face and heard the people's comments in the street. They'd have seen the local newspaper placards, constantly reminding residents of the city that *Titanic* was no more. They would have asked whether their father would be coming back but Emily wouldn't have been able to answer. Indeed, by 18 April, so many questions were still unanswered and the queues at the White Star Line offices continued to grow. All through that afternoon, people kept on coming. Some were anxious, others were men striving to keep a stiff upper lip and others were sobbing wives desperate simply to know the fate of their husbands or sons. The reporting in the local papers continued with all the touching minutiae of a novel, with clerks emerging from the White Star Offices at regular intervals, only to announce there was still no news and the subsequent reactions on the faces in the crowd. The waiting women tried desperately to keep each other's spirits up. One moving report in the *Southern Daily Echo* reads:

> "'Tom's sure to be all right,' one sympathetic neighbour sought to console a friend, "he was always one of the lucky ones." The other woman shook her head sadly but with a gesture of pride. "I know he's gone," she answered in a hushed whisper of conviction, "but I know my Tom would do his duty."'

But what was the 'duty' that this wife spoke of? What exactly was expected of the *Titanic*'s crew? They were not all Royal Navy sailors, trained in lifesaving and rescue missions, but normal crew on a passenger liner – stewards, stokers, chefs, waiters. Some were mere boys. Some had not even been to sea before. True, their duty as crew would have been to aid and assist passengers as much as possible. But to die in their place? Was that their duty? Already it seemed, even before the deaths were confirmed, the general rhetoric became one of 'duty' and of 'sacrifice' and that the crew who had died had done so giving up their right to live for their betters. It was as if these working-class crew members were on board not only to heave coal into furnaces or to clean up after aristocrats or to serve the well-off, but also to lay down their lives if necessary for those richer, more powerful, more deserving of the right to survive. But there were already angry murmurings as news reached home that there had not been enough lifeboats. Why had there not been enough? Why had most of the rich survived while the poor perished? Angry talk began between some, while others, such as this waiting wife, felt the fatalistic knowledge that certain lives' outcomes are already decided. Rich would survive, poor would die instead of them. It is a poignant reminder of the views of class at the time; of how some lives were worth far more than others while other lives were cheap and disposable.

By 18 April, family members were becoming impatient for news. Sobbing women pushed to the front of the crowds, asking the constables on duty outside the White Star Line offices if there was any news or any hope. Some women were insistent that they must know something inside. But the reply was as ever – No news yet. This lack of news, of confirmation, the closed door with occasional bulletins of 'nothing yet', must have been infuriating and agonising in equal measure. The famous British 'stiff upper lip' that the papers had so proudly reported thus far began to crumble away. 'Women clung to each other for support,' reported the *Southern Daily Echo*, 'intertwining their hands and arms or bit their twisted handkerchiefs to keep from sobbing. Occasionally there was an exclamation of thankfulness: "Thank God, he's saved." This, unfortunately, was the exception.' My father told me that his mother said Emily had waited too at the White Star Line offices. She'd waited in the hope of seeing William's name. But she never did find a name on a list outside the White Star Line offices. During the days she waited, she must have seen women and other wives she recognized stumbling back from the front of the queue in tears. But she still must have hoped there might be some chance William's name would be added to the survivors' list. She waited. But his name never materialized.

Alongside the news reports of sobbing women and queues of ever-hopeful relatives, came the interviews with the people who were supposed to have sailed on *Titanic* but had 'premonitions' or omens that they should not go. One conversation was reported in the *Southampton Times*:

> 'You may not believe in dreams, but Mrs Slade I am telling you the truth when I say that one of my boys had a dream about the boat the night before the sailing day and he afterwards said that he had a dread of her. I knew they were not very keen on going, but nevertheless they went down.'

Other tales abounded of crew having dreams the night before sailing, of picture frames falling to the floor the night of the tragedy, of elderly sages telling others that the fact *Titanic* had a delayed sailing because of nearly colliding with the *New York* in Southampton the day she set sail – all were omens that something dark and tragic was to come. It is easy to look back to a tragedy of this scale and read portents into every 'sign'. In my own family, even years after the tragedy, relatives spoke of how William was not supposed to have been on board and had taken his job at the last minute. This added aspect that Fate played a role in these men's deaths only adds to the mystique of the *Titanic* disaster. Others too had their fates decided at the very last minute.

A family descendant of Alfred Geer, a stoker who died on *Titanic*, told me that her great-uncle had just finished working on the ship *Olympic* but was out of work when *Titanic* steamed in to Southampton. Linda Gregory explained to me how during the coal shortage, Alfred Geer would stand at the docks with other men, waiting and hoping to be taken on for more work. She told me:

> 'He and five other *Olympic* crewmen were on the dockside at Southampton looking for work, when they were spotted and informed that a gang of six men who were coming from Ireland had failed to turn up and their positions were available. My great-uncle and the others took up those positions. It transpired that the men who had failed to turn up had gone drinking and were too inebriated to get there.'

So many *Titanic* crew stories' outcomes were on a knife-edge. Fate. Accident. Coincidence. A drink that lasted too long in a pub, being too late, having someone else take your place. There was often talk of 'what ifs' – what if he hadn't taken the job, what if someone else had got there a few minutes before him …What if …One widow, Mrs May, was interviewed in the *Daily Mail*. She lost her husband and her son on the ship and in her own words the menfolk had 'left eleven of us.' She already began, understandably, to seek someone or something to blame. She said:

> 'It was the first time that Arthur and his father had been at sea together and it wouldn't have happened if Arthur hadn't been out of work because of the coal strike. He tried to get a job ashore but failed and he had his wife and baby to keep. So he signed on aboard the *Titanic* as a fireman.'

Mrs May's lamentations were not the hysterics of a grief-stricken widow. They were well founded. If there had not been a coal strike, the men would not have been so desperate or so poor. *Titanic* had arrived in Southampton at the tail end of a national coal strike, offering jobs at exactly the moment the poorest workers needed them most. After she sank, those grieving now understandably needed to make sense of it all by finding a cause for the effect. The coal strike ... an omen ... a portentous dream. *What if. What if.* It must have been even harder for Emily to accept; hearing these tales of omens and premonitions and knowing that if her William had been just a little later to seek work that day, or been beaten to the post by a younger, fitter man, he might not have sailed at all. He would still be alive.

Of course, there were miracle stories that shone out among the gloom and despair. One son had been grieving that his father, a steward on the *Titanic*, was dead but then received a cable that he had been saved. Jackie Ward, the steward's son, ran into the *Southern Daily Echo* newspaper offices shouting, 'Please, I've got a cable from my dad. He's saved!' But Jackie Ward's story was a rare one. For most children and wives, there was still no news. Even the national newspapers such as the *Daily Mail* wrote of the difficulty of obtaining concrete answers about the number of survivors or, indeed, what had even happened:

> 'Seldom indeed has a more thrilling tale been told to the people of two continents than that of the strange accident to the White Star liner *Titanic*, which all day and night was coming in by instalments, as the wireless messages sped over the waters of the Atlantic from the stricken ship and the vessels which she had called up to her rescue. Their alternate burden of dismay and hope held the world in suspense.'

This 'alternate burden of dismay and hope' was further augmented by the fact that there were so many mix ups. One such mix up was told to me by the descendant of Percival Albert Blake, a coal trimmer on *Titanic*. My social media searches led me to his descendant, who explained that initially Percival's name was wrongly posted on a list of those who had died. His parents, Edwin and Clara Blake, and his sister Millie had waited to see this list. When they saw his name confirmed with the names of the dead they went home and began mourning their loss. But days later, his descendant told me, Percy's name was then added to the list of survivors. There had been a mix up and he was not dead at all. The jump for his family from despair and grief to sheer elation in a matter of days is hard to imagine. His descendant kindly sent me a photograph of Percy taken on his arrival to safety in

New York. This pictorial evidence confirms he did indeed make it. In his bowler hat and smart suit – no doubt donated or lent as he would have had no clothing or belongings after the sinking – Percival looks every inch the hopeful New York immigrant on the brink of new life, rather than a man who just cheated death and survived one of the sea's greatest ever tragedies. For my great-grandmother, though, there was no mix up, nor was there concrete confirmation. William's name was never posted on the survivors' list. Nor did she find him on a list of the dead. Like so many other wives, mothers and fiancées around the city, she was in limbo; waiting for good news or bad. It was the no news that was so agonizing. But in the meantime, while there was no news, she had to survive. It is at this point, so my aunt tells me, that Emily made the decision to start taking in washing to earn money. She would have been no stranger to doing the family's endless washing in a copper bath but now she took in neighbours' laundry to survive. Taking in washing was something very poor women did, of course, and it was seen as being on the same level as having to resort to pawning your belongings in those days. It means Emily must have been desperate. Shame or embarrassment didn't matter now. She had to earn money even though she had no idea where William was. Dead or alive, nothing had changed. Her children still had to eat.

By 20 April, people began to give up all hope. The crowds, that had been so large for the last few days, began to fade away. Only a few people now bothered to gather outside the White Star Line offices on Canute Road. The *Southern Daily Echo* summed it up:

> 'The worst fears of many a wife, mother and child were realised yesterday and a deep gloom has settled over the streets wherein the seafaring population have their homes – a gloom no longer relieved by a ray of hope.'

The hope may have faded but the tragedy was already attracting sympathy from the world over. *Titanic* really was the first international tragedy to be reported on such a scale. As the *Daily Graphic wrote*:

> 'We trust the relatives of those who perished may find some solace in the thought that though they have been called upon to suffer a grief almost unendurable to bear, they

suffer it amidst that deepest sympathy which only when we are brought to face the realities of life can be aroused … Millionaire and steerage emigrant alike were called upon: alike they have presented us with that most inspiring of all spectacles – the inherent nobility of mankind.'

It was only five days since *Titanic* had foundered and already those who had perished were being beatified, while those left behind and grieving were being written about with an almost religious reverence. The purple prose may well have been well meant but it would not aid the hungry children and desperate wives whose husbands' boots were still in the pawnbrokers' windows. It was true that being a wife whose crewmember husband had died meant she could hold her head high that he 'did his duty' in sacrificing his life. But that pride would not pay the rent or feed the hungry children. Emily didn't have time to lap up the national and international sympathy; she needed an income. But while she and other women like her pawned their few possessions and took in washing, help was on its way. The Mayor of Southampton, Councillor Henry Bowyer, was already in talks to set up a relief fund. He began discussions with the Lord Mayor of London to set up a fund for the relief of those who would suffer by the loss of the *Titanic*. In fact, his personal heartfelt message to the Lord Mayor of London was printed in the *Southern Daily Echo* in which he proposed to open a relief fund for the 'distressed dependants' of the *Titanic* crew, 'the majority of whom reside in Southampton…' The British Seafarers' Union was also advising wives and other dependants that they were entitled to compensation. The secretary of the Union announced that the dependants of each Union member were entitled to £5 death benefit and added, 'Under the amended Workmen's Compensation Act seamen – in which term are included all the hands working on the ship – come under the provisions of the Act, and their relatives will receive compensation in due course.'

Until that time, though, life had to go on. The *Titanic* wives agonised over whether their husbands were truly dead or alive and how to feed their families. The children, already used to hunger and meagre rations, simply grieved. Northam Girls' School recorded in its log:

'April 17th – I feel I must record the sad aspect in school today owing to the 'Titanic' disaster. So many of the crew belong to Northam and it is pathetic to witness the children's grief; and in some cases faith and hope of better news. The attendance is suffering…'

Other schools reported absent or grieving children, too:

'April 22nd – 12 scholars have been rendered fatherless owing to the terrible Titanic disaster: nine stewards, one store keeper and one butcher all reported missing. As far as can be ascertained 30 children have lost relatives.'[2]

Across the city, many children stayed home from school, too upset to go – or perhaps they had no boots to go to school with, their desperate parents having pawned them for a few coins. Others might have been ill with diphtheria, which was common. Others would go to school for the day before heading off down to the dock gates to see if their fathers' names might have been added on to the list of survivors, as one resident recalled of the time:

'[a friend] her father got lost…they put names up…outside the dock gates…who was rescued and that…This girl at school…she used to come and say: "Coming down the dock gate?" Me and my sister used to go down the dock gate to see if her father's name was up there. Several girls at the school, that had fathers on there…well, brothers or some relation.'[3]

Everyone, it seemed had either lost someone they knew, or knew someone who had. And if children didn't have boots *before* the *Titanic* tragedy, now things were about to get worse. With widows desperately trying to afford to feed their families, many children had to go without other necessities, such as clothes. In Northam Girls' School log on May 7, 1912, it is recorded, 'I have distributed clothes to the children who were bereft through the 'Titanic' disaster.' A couple of miles away in Freemantle, the Freemantle C of E Boys' School recorded in their log that they had sent in the names of two boys at the school who had lost fathers in the sinking 'for consideration by Distress Committee.'

But already, donations were pouring in – not just in Britain but from around the world. It was reported in the *Hampshire Independent* on

20 April that the Mayor of Southampton had a 'phenomenally heavy letter bag containing letters of sympathy and practical offers of help from all over the world.' Donations were made from far and wide and benefit performances were planned, including at the Hippodrome, Southampton. Orphanages from around Britain also made contact, offering to take in any orphans who had neither mother or father after the tragedy. In the days after *Titanic* sank, full columns in the local papers were devoted simply to listing the hundreds of names of people who were donating money, and the amounts they were declaring they'd donate. And prominent voices were speaking out, expressing their sorrow and condolences. One of those was Captain Smith's wife. Just as stokers, trimmers, engineers and stewards had lost their lives, so had the great man himself: Captain Smith had gone down with his ship and was being spoken about with hushed reverence. His wife, Sarah Eleanor Smith, wrote a letter to the local paper. 'To my fellow sufferers, my heart overflows with grief for all of you,' she wrote. 'May God be with you and comfort you all. Eleanor Smith.' Her words, as the 'chief wife' of the mourning widows, must have been a great comfort. To poor women like my great-grandmother, reading Captain Smith's wife's words at their kitchen table must have been a soothing balm; showing that even women at the elevated heights of Captain's wife were sharing the grief of the poorest widow.

In fact, it would have been hard for Emily not to feel the empathy and true understanding from the women all around her, because, as the newspapers were reporting, there was scarcely a family that had not lost a loved one. The very streets seemed to ooze grief and despair and 'children returned from school appreciated something of tragedy, and woeful little faces were turned to the darkened, fatherless homes.'[4]

There were hundreds in dark, fatherless homes in Southampton. My grandmother, Florence, and her four siblings made up part of this number. Families went into mourning. Children who had previously played with a ball or with their hoops in the street stayed behind closed doors. It went quiet. Another resident recalled the effect the loss of *Titanic* had on the city: 'A great hush descended on the town because I don't think there was hardly a single street in Southampton who hadn't lost somebody on that ship...' This interviewee went on to recount that there was little help at first for women and orphans and how there were charity concerts later in the same year 'in aid of the widows and orphans'.[5]

The generous donations continued to come in. Theatres promised to donate percentages of their takings to the Relief Fund. Even private local companies offered help, with one advert in the *Hampshire Independent* from furniture company F. Baker and Sons offering 'free conveyancing of furniture' to the *Titanic* widows 'irrespective of the amount owing.' Papers reported that this must have been a comfort and that the great national and international whip-round must have started to relieve the distress of the bereaved. But I wonder how true that was at that point. The relief fund would take time to set up and, while they waited, the widows must survive. All the ordinary, everyday events of the time still had to be dealt with. Some children were ill with consumption and diphtheria and other illnesses such as measles were still doing the rounds.[6]

Older children who had been in the middle of low-paid apprenticeships now had to worry about how their continuing education would be supported without a father's income. But aside from these concerns people also needed to grieve; to remember and acknowledge their loved one who had drowned. On 20 April, a memorial service was held at St Mary's Church, Southampton, in memory of the crew who had perished. It was a grand affair; the Bishop of Winchester addressed the congregation, the mayor was present, along with consular officials, shipping company managers and, of course, sailors, residents and wives and children. One rather renowned wife was there too – Captain Smith's wife. In his sermon, reported in the *Southern Daily Echo* of a few days later, the Bishop said:

> 'In spite of the glory of the spring and sunshine streaming in, there is a pall of sorrow all over the country, which lay thicker over Southampton. None could remember a catastrophe so awful.'

He also told the congregation that God had meant that this 'should be so' and that those who had died 'had to die at some time' which sounds perhaps rather flippant and callous to us today but this was smoothed over when he added that 'God had His ways in the catastrophes of the world.' He then added sombrely that the disaster was a mighty lesson against people's trust in machinery – and money. *Titanic*, wrote the local paper, 'would stand as a monument of warning against human presumption.'

That human presumption was that, as the biggest manmade object on the planet as well as being the most opulent and beautiful, *Titanic* would never sink. That is why so many were still in stunned shock. *Titanic* was representative of all that was technological and successful of the age; of man's ability to control nature. This wasn't supposed to have happened. Reports would later suggest that some people refused their place in lifeboats because they simply felt safer on board, sinking or not. They, like everyone else, could not believe that *Titanic* could end this way. But man had failed and nature had won. Other memorial services were held all over the city and all over the country and the world. On 19 April, a memorial service was held in St Paul's Cathedral in London which housed a 'vast crowd of men and women, moved by an emotion as poignant as unshed tears.'[7] Reports extolled the fact that people of all classes and backgrounds came together to share their grief over *Titanic* and that the tragedy had 'made our brotherhood close its ranks like little children who cling together in fear and grief.' As evidence of how huge the disaster was at the time, King George sent a telegram to the President of the United States expressing his sorrow at the loss of life both among American citizens and his own subjects. Likewise, President Taft replied expressing how the American people shared in the sorrow of 'their kinsmen beyond the sea.'

On 29 April, a massive memorial service was held, this time at the Marlands area of Southampton. Tens of thousands attended, desperate to get some kind of comfort in a sermon, or a Biblical reference, or a heartfelt hymn. But all the while these families could not even go through the steps that they knew so well about grief and death. Death was an everyday occurrence to poor people in 1912. Diphtheria, consumption and even 'flu epidemics would take many poor lives. But perhaps because death was such an everyday occurrence, there were rules and norms that were always followed so strictly. But now they could not be. Flags were at half mast, shutters and blinds were closed in many streets to show respect, church services were held to honour the dead. But all these wives and mothers wanted was the one thing missing – a body over which to grieve. Funeral rites and fashions at this period in history were unwavering. There wasn't much worse than a pauper's burial. But without a body to bring home, to watch over, to say goodbye to and then to follow to the church, how could these early twentieth century people grieve? It's perhaps easy to think that because poor people in 1912 would have been far more used to death than we are today that they didn't grieve as deeply. My great-grandmother and her contemporaries mourning their drowned husbands were trapped between the 'culture of death' of Victorian times – the perhaps macabre, by our standards, 'celebration' of death – and the quieter, more reflective reaction to death which seemed to coincide with the advent of the First World War. But working-class people grieved very much indeed. Historians have recounted how some poor children would 'play at funerals',[8] arguably because these working-class children were so used to seeing death in their families. But a familiarity with death doesn't mean it hurts any less. In other words, although their poverty meant these people saw death every day, they didn't grieve any less. Poverty, desperation and the struggle to survive did not exempt my great-grandmother and her fellow widows from grief. And there were rites and norms and funereal processes that had to be observed, for society's sake – such as a proper Christian burial and not a pauper's. But without a body to perform these rites upon, these wives and mothers must have felt lost, bereft, unable to move through that grief. It didn't aid matters that there was no concrete answer as to whether many husbands or sons were truly dead or alive. 'Lost at sea' is the standard phrase meaning the worst. But that phrase is also ambiguous. Lost things can be found again. People can turn up. For those clinging to hope, the word 'lost' was preferable to 'dead.'

Emily's situation was not unique. It was being replicated all over the city. Wives of stewards, firemen, trimmers and able seamen still had no idea whether their husbands were dead or might just turn up. Rose Puzey, whose descendant Mike Knowlton kindly provided me with copies of letters she received, waited in vain to hear of her steward husband John. Just months earlier they'd had a happy family photograph taken. Now she was waiting to hear if her husband was alive or dead. And then, on 22 May, Rose received a letter from the Finance Department which read:

> 'I am directed by the Board of Trade to inform you that your claim to the Wages of J.E Puzey a deceased seaman, having been admitted, an Order in your favour has been transmitted to the Superintendent of the Mercantile Marine Office at the Port of Southampton to whom you should make application, either personally or by letter, and by whom any certificates, letters, &c, forwarded in support of claim will be returned.'[9]

This would have been the first written confirmation for Rose that her husband was a 'deceased' seaman. And a month later, on 20 June, another letter arrived. This letter, from the General Register and Record Office of Shipping and Seamen read, 'Madam, In compliance with your request received the 4th instant, I forward herewith a certified Extract relating to the supposed death of JE Puzey late of the Titanic.' The word 'supposed' was added by hand. Rose and John's family member told me that when she did receive some monies some weeks later from her husband's wages, the powers that be had deducted the cost of his uniform.

Then there were the women who were in limbo but also pregnant. There was the case of Florence Jones, the wife of Harry Jones who had signed on to Titanic as a roast cook. Harry had already survived the collision incident on the RMS Olympic when she was struck by Hawke and had always joked to friends and family that his ship would 'turn turtle.' His prophecy came true on Titanic. His body was never found. But Florence had been pregnant when he'd set sail and later gave birth to a son in October 1912. Widowed and with no breadwinner she had a new baby to bring up who would never meet his father.

Another woeful story was that of Arthur Herbert Morgan who had signed on to Titanic as a trimmer. It was his first ever ship. He was married to Eleanor Earley and they had had a son, Francis, who had died a year earlier in 1911 aged only two. For Eleanor to lose her toddler son must have been an enormous blow but now it was confirmed that her husband, aged only 27, had died in the Titanic disaster. One can only struggle to imagine her sense of loss and despair, still grieving for their two-year-old and now too over the loss of her young husband. It was Arthur Morgan's parents who placed a memorial in the local paper: MORGAN--April 15th, at sea, on s.s. Titanic, Arthur Herbert, age 27, the second son of Caroline and the late Charles Morgan, of 121 Bevois Street, Southampton. Gone but not forgotten.' There was a further tragedy to come for the family, which I will refer to later. Other memorials from the time make for sorrowful reading. 'Abrams – April 15th, as on Titanic, in fond and loving memory of my dear Daddy...' was one. Another read: Ahier – April 15th, at sea, on SS Titanic, Percy Snowden Ahier, the dearly loved son of John and Clara...' and, tragically, 'Barratt – April 15th 1912, in loving memory of Arthur, the deeply beloved son of Arthur and Margaret Barratt...who died at sea in the wreck of the Titanic, aged 15 years.'[10] Arthur would by our standards be considered just a boy but he too had lost his life. But in the eyes of those around him in 1912, he was very much a man, having been to sea before as a bellboy and bringing home earnings of £2 on *Titanic*. He was the Barratts's only son. The sheer scale of this sense of loss – even for the very poor who must be 'used' to death – was not un-noted in the world's press.

> 'Sadder than death itself was the pity which went out to those who lived to mourn – to the young widows who were tired of weeping, to the mothers who had lost their sons, to men who had lost their comrades. Not within living memory has any tragedy so stirred the heart and conscience of the world. In Southampton, from which nearly all the crew had gone, there was a piteous lamentation.'[11]

But amongst the gloom and the spectre of death that the world's press was writing about, there were of course survivors. And in Southampton, relatives, journalists and the general public could not wait to welcome them home. On 29 April, of the 165 rescued members of the crew, 85 arrived at Southampton railway station. They'd been rescued and brought back to Britain on the SS *Lapland* which had docked at Plymouth. Now they were home. Wives and mothers and sweethearts all congregated at the railway station eager to greet their men. The local paper reported 'affecting scenes' as well as 'thrilling narratives' and interviewed one unnamed fireman who had survived. This no-doubt exhausted, relieved, grateful colleague of my great-grandfather gave an impromptu interview as he stepped off the train in which he explained the events of the night *Titanic* hit the iceberg. This fireman explained how the watertight compartments had closed and every man had stood at his post. He explained to journalists how the chief engineer Mr Bell ordered the firemen to draw the fires presumably to prevent an explosion and that the men continued to do this until 'the water was up to their waists.' This man said that when the firemen couldn't stay at their posts any longer, their superiors told them to 'go aboard.' This man explained to the press that the reason so many firemen had been saved was because there was only one watch on duty when *Titanic* hit the iceberg. 'The next watch were prepared to go down for their spell of duty when the disaster happened, in fact,' said the narrator, who was in this section, 'we had just got into our stokehold gear which, as you know, consists merely of trousers, flannel shirt and boots and that was all we had to take our plunge into the water…'[12]

My great-grandfather would have been in 'the next watch', preparing to go to work. I've no doubt my great-grandmother would have read every single local and national report on the disaster she could get her hands on. It is hard to imagine how she must have felt reading this particular interview with a man who would have been colleagues with her husband; a man who did the same exhausting job, for the same pay, but for some unknown reason had been lucky. He'd survived. She must have wondered where William had been at the moment of impact. Had he been one of the men this fireman had spoken of, standing waist-deep in freezing water, trying desperately to keep the ship afloat as long as possible? Hearing the description of the uniform of flannel shirt and trousers must have brought back domestic memories of washing the godforsaken clothes many times. But it would have also made her grief all the more real; knowing that William would have been in the same clothing, freezing, terrified, hopeless. She must have also felt a bitter-sweet sensation of joy and relief for the women she knew whose husbands did come home on that train to Southampton, as well as an acrid, dark, sorrowful envy that her husband was not one of them.

My great-grandfather's name never did turn up on a list. Instead, so my aunt tells me, a few days after the tragedy there was a knock at the door in Henry Road. It was the bearer of a letter. In it, it was confirmed that William Edward Bessant, fireman on RMS *Titanic*, was lost at sea, aged 40. In this household, there had been no mix up but there was not a body to confirm a death either. Yet, it was official. William would not be coming home. I've often imagined the scene where my great-grandmother was told her husband was lost on the *Titanic*. Was she doing the street's laundry, her sleeves rolled up and her forearms red-raw? Was she making some meagre meal for her five children? I've wondered countless times how she was told. Did she usher the children out of the room? Or did they stand around her skirts, peering up at her and waiting for her reaction? I've often wondered whether she cried or held it together; whether she fainted or carried on looking after her children. Grief itself must have been bad enough. Losing a husband is terrible whatever era you are living in. But to lose a husband who was the only means of eating, of keeping a roof over your head and your children in school boots must have been utterly shattering. Before she could sit down and weep that she'd lost her husband of almost 20 years; the man she'd taken a chance on, leaving the farmlands where her family lived and worked, she first must have had to make calculations. Could they pay the rent for the rest of this month? Could they afford to eat? Would the children have to stop attending school? Despite her many practical and financial worries, despite no body to weep over and no grave to visit, Emily was strong enough to explain it all to her children and tell them their father would not be coming home. She then mustered more strength to be able to place a death notice in the *Hampshire Independent* days later on 4 May, which read: 'William Edward Bessant. Dearly beloved husband of Emily Bessant, of 5, Henry Road, Freemantle. God be with you until we meet again…'

If this were a film, our camera would zoom out now from Henry Road where my great-grandmother lived, leaving a lingering scene. The rooms where the children slept are in darkness but there is a faint light coming from the window of the front room downstairs. A figure sits hunched over a table. She has her head in her hands. It is at this point that I believe my stoical, hard, steely-eyed great-grandmother let herself do something she had needed to do since April 15.

Weep.

Chapter 4

Survival

The temperature in Southampton County Court was 'tropical' and so His Honour Judge Gye took his seat without his usual wig and gown. It was July 1912, and, as well as the temperature rising, so was the sense of agitation. The hearing in question was that of the *Titanic* cases. When the *Titanic* sank, the White Star Line suspended payments to crew. At first, the company would not pay any compensation for the loss of crew members at all. Even their meagre pay was suspended. The crew had been promised half pay during the voyage and half when it was completed. Pay stopped, therefore, when the ship went down. For a little, ordinary person who lived in a two-up, two-down to take on a giant like the White Star Line was an enormous undertaking. But already, these little ordinary people were seeking recompense – even against a colossal force who believed its ship unsinkable. Grief and desperation fuelled them. This was more than a terrible tragedy. It was now about rich versus poor. The statistics that we know now speak for themselves; 60 per cent of the first class passengers survived, whereas over 70 per cent of the crew died. They had done their 'duty', whatever that was, but now their families needed compensating. Judge Gye sat in the oven-like court room and listened to 60 cases presented on behalf of *Titanic* crew widows seeking compensation under the Workmen's Compensation Act. A month earlier, the White Star Line had made payments for compensation claims into the County Court and the amounts to be awarded were already decided: a maximum per dependant of £300 on the strict basis of £294 15s per leading fireman; the same amount per greaser; £237 12s per ordinary fireman; £223 15s per trimmer. It's no small wonder the atmosphere in the courtroom was heated. This was not a paltry sum on offer to these people. This would have been life-changing money. The maximum award given to wives such as my great-grandmother – a fireman's wife – would equate to £22,400 in today's money. Of course, not everyone would receive anywhere near the maximum amount. It had at first seemed so straightforward – those who had lost a husband or provider could now be compensated. Yet earlier in the month, Judge Gye had presided over a court hearing – this time in less balmy circumstances and properly dressed in his wig and gown – in which he had had to differentiate between those who were truly 'dependants' and those who were not. In that hearing, Judge Gye had sat before a court room of ladies in 'deep mourning' and was presented with the case of a mother who had claimed to be a dependant of a *Titanic* crewman victim and had therefore claimed her compensation of £294, 16s but it had been discovered that she had not received any money from her son for eight years and was, therefore, not dependent. Exasperated Judge Gye addressed the court room saying, 'There are a great many ideas abroad which are wholly fallacious.' To which solicitor Mr C.A. Emmanuel replied, 'Just the same as they all think they are entitled to £300 when they are not.'

It was not an easy process for the widows or dependants. Women had to give evidence under oath. In one case, a widow fainted after giving evidence and had to be assisted by the St John's Ambulance Association. Other widows broke down in tears and several asked for their money to be paid in a lump sum so that they could buy furniture as they were forced go to into lodging houses. These women had only lost their husbands a matter of weeks ago but they had to stand before a court, take an oath and give evidence as to whether they had children or not. In many cases, half a sum was allotted to the widow and the other half to her children – if they were very young. If the children were older, the award would be divided as one third to the widow and two thirds 'placed to the credit of the children.'

How the money would be paid depended on the circumstances of the widow. In some cases, her award was paid out monthly, often at £4 a month. In other cases, when women wanted to start a business or move abroad, larger sums were paid out. Other widows asked that their award should not be paid out now but invested instead. Others, who were in debt, came forward asking if the payments included or excluded their husbands' debts to which Judge Gye replied that compensation should be received by 'dependants, and should be free from the debts of the deceased.' ' It was also noted in court by Judge Gye that these widows already had vultures circling around them, saying that many who found a 'poor widow with a good round sum immediately took steps to get hold of it' and that the widows needed 'very careful protection'. Emily Bessant's surname is mentioned in newspaper copy in the courts at the time but there is no record of how much compensation she actually received.

Debts. Compensation. Investments. Two months had passed since the loss of *Titanic* and, although women still grieved very deeply for their lost husbands or sons, now the focus was very much on surviving fiscally. Distant relatives who had never even relied on their deceased relative's earnings from his seafaring work came forward to seek compensation – and were told a firm no. Some women used the money to carry on surviving. Others had entrepreneurial ideas of investing in shops or businesses and sought advice. For people who had lived hand to mouth all their lives in flooded slum housing or unable to send their children to school in boots, this money would change lives. It's no wonder so many were seeking compensation – whether they were direct dependants or not.

But who can blame them? Poverty clung to the widows and dependants of *Titanic*'s crew in Southampton as the sea mists so often clung to the boats. After *Titanic* foundered, poor families found themselves even more destitute than ever. Before, they were poor, but they at least had some money coming in when the breadwinner was at sea. Now they were utterly destitute. There was no pay to claim, no wage brought home. The women talked in the street, hungry, worried, offering each other an ear, coming up with strategies of how to survive another few days. This affected the children, of course, and many more now needed free school meals or had no boots in which to walk to school with. 'The acute distress among the people is daily becoming more evident,' recorded the writer in Northam Girls' School log, '24 free meals given today and the shoeless hungry children are many.' Until the Relief Fund awards were given, local people rallied round to help the poor widows. The National Union of Ships' Stewards, Butchers and Bakers had also started a fund and would grant £2 per member for their immediate survival.

There were also charity matinees to 'relieve the sufferings of widows and children', sports events, collections in the streets and promenade charity concerts. Southampton alone raised £41,000 towards the Titanic Relief Fund. If these women were seen as the wives of lowly firemen before, now they were elevated to an almost saintly station in their suffering and newspapers wrote of the stoical, brave women who had to carry on without their men. But the reality was that until her award was given, Emily Bessant couldn't do much with sympathy, however well meant. She carried on taking in washing and stood at her copper bath day and night, hands burnt and raw. She also still had to get her children to school, to clothe them, to feed them, as well as doing the household chores. All without an income. Perhaps neighbours and friends took pity and would bring her some eggs or flour or other basics. But she needed a long-term plan. Did she up sticks and move her family back to the rural farmlands where she came from? Did she leave the city behind and every grim, dark memory? Or did she stay and fight – as perhaps William would have wanted her to? Her eldest son Charles stepped up to be man of the house, taking on more errand work while the children went back to school and tried to carry on. Young people – considered teenagers today – now had to grow up overnight and take charge. Elsewhere, other younger children carried on as well.

Amy Willsher was just one such child. Her father William, an assistant butcher, had died on *Titanic*. Amy, then aged nine, was the youngest child to lose a father at Northam Girls' School and was presented with a doll donated by the Fourth Avenue Girls' School in Manor Park, London. Children all over the city would have been in similar circumstances, still trying to focus at school, still hungry, still wondering where their father was. These children would have been what we would now describe as 'traumatized'. They would not only have lost their fathers, but they would have seen their mothers frantically trying to claim money that was rightfully theirs, to try to keep food on the table. And all the while, these children would have been grieving with none of the services we take for granted today such as counselling, talking therapies and support. Perhaps the children who lost fathers comforted each other. At least they would have understood what the other was going through.

Schools also were financially generous to families who had lost fathers. School logs from the time detail many local schools raising money from the children themselves to donate to those who had lost fathers, with the All Saints Boys School collecting £2 6s 8d. The school log of 15 May records that 'Every boy on the register subscribed and was requested to give some of his own money, and not to ask his parents or anyone for money to give to the fund.' These teachers knew not to ask adults for funds because many were already so poor, perhaps even only a few steps away from the workhouse. It is testament to the generosity and the strength of feeling in the city that young children all donated to help other scholars like themselves. Meanwhile, the need of the women left behind was urgent. The Southampton Slum Officers visited the homes of hundreds of dependants of *Titanic* crew and found virtually every other house in mourning. The suffering of those left behind was immense and was detailed in the Salvation Army magazine *War Cry*:

'The work of ministering to the sufferers is women's work. This is true, whether it be Adjutants Clark, Groome, and Marsh and Lieutenant Mils, the Officers of Battenberg Home for Women and Girls who supply hundreds of quarts of soup or milk to the needy, or the Slum Officers who deliver many gallons of milk to nursing mothers and children and take gifts of tea, bread, sugar, rice and other provender to the homes where the grim spectre of want as long been seen and where the shadow of death has now fallen.'[1]

The shadow of death might well have fallen on the humble homes and slums in Southampton but national newspapers, such as the *Daily Mail*, were doing their journalistic duty and were already totalling up the amount the White Star Company might have to relinquish in compensation, describing its 'heavy liabilities'. 'Assuming that 700 of the crew whose relatives can claim have been lost, and that compensation reaches an amount of £200 a head on the average, that would involve a further £140,000,' wrote the Daily Mail. Further fuel was added to the fire in other reports that Captain Smith had earned the 'exceptionally large' salary of £1,250 a year and that chief officers generally earned £14 to £20 per month. The White Star Line had an insurance and pension scheme for these senior crew members and the *Mail* reported that Captain Smith's wife would receive £1,168 as his widow. Any other crew on board whose total earnings did not amount to £250 would be covered by the Workmen's Compensation Act. The act, passed in 1906, protected low paid workers and their rights for seeking compensation for injury.

Meanwhile, passengers' families too sought compensation. Early 'test' cases were brought. In July 1912, the White Star Company held a committee meeting in which it was announced that £288 had been paid into court for the case of the dependants of A.D Nichols, third class steward. Another early case was that of Thomas Ryan versus the Oceanic Steam Navigation Company (or White Star Line). Thomas Ryan's son Patrick had been a third-class passenger onboard *Titanic* and had drowned. Thomas Ryan brought a suit against White Star claiming negligence based on facts such as that *Titanic* was going too fast, that they had failed to supply their look-out men with binoculars and that there had not been adequate lifeboats available. This was a test case – and one that was watched eagerly by both relatives of deceased passengers and crew. Thomas Ryan claimed on the basis that his son had been a cattle dealer earning £2 a week and that he, Thomas, was a dependant. He won his case and was awarded £100 for the loss of his son. Many of the widows and dependants of crew who died on *Titanic* would not have known how or where to seek advice, or even have dreamed they might be eligible to bring a suit. So they did not. Some still longed to find a place they could grieve – a grave.

One such person was Emily Wormald whose husband Frederick Henry Wormald, a first-class saloon steward, had died on *Titanic*. Unlike many of the lost crew who were simply 'lost at sea', Frederick Wormald's body had been picked up by the cable ship *Mackay-Bennett* – the ship tasked with the grim job of bringing bodies to land – and taken to Halifax, Nova Scotia. His body was laid out with others to be identified – at the rather unfitting location of a curling rink. But a local rabbi had apparently wrongly identified Frederick as Jewish and his body was taken off to a Jewish cemetery and interred there. When Emily Wormald heard of this, she expressed her wish to visit her husband's grave. The White Star Line, out of kindness or perhaps for positive public relations purposes, put Emily Wormald and her six children on the *St Louis* – a ship on which Frederick had worked previously – to sail to New York and then make their way to Canada to visit Frederick's grave. Mrs Wormald gave her next door neighbour Mrs Eustace as her 'nearest friend' when boarding the ship and sailed on 24 August 1912. No one can know what Mrs Wormald's true reasons were for the huge journey to visit her dead husband's grave. Was she just visiting the grave? Did she feel compelled to find a place to feel closer to her husband? Or was she planning a new life in a new world at a time of great uncertainty? Either way, immigration officials at New York were not convinced of Mrs Wormald's pilgrimage to the grave story. She was taken to Ellis Island for immigration check purposes and, instead of welcoming poor grieving Mrs Wormald, the authorities there refused her and her family entry and promptly put them all back on the ship. The passage took days and the family finally arrived back in Southampton on 15 September. The trip must have been exhausting, not to mention embarrassing and humiliating. Thankfully, other passengers and crew on board her return journey had felt sorry for her and had done a whip-round for her of £40. But when Mrs Wormald, no doubt exhausted, tired and in need of a long sleep, returned to her rented home in Southampton, she stood in the street, stunned. Her landlord – perhaps thinking she was not coming back – had re-let her family home to another family, dumping her furniture and possessions in the street. Her friend and neighbour Mrs Eustace had done her best, keeping as much of the Wormalds' furniture and possessions for them in her upstairs rooms. But Mrs Wormald was now not only a widow. She was a homeless widow. She was put up in a mission hall nearby and then found another house to rent.[2] It seems unfeeling now for a widow to be treated this way by the American immigration authorities – and by her own landlord. However, at an earlier court hearing (presided over by on-off-wig-wearing Judge Gye) the case had been heard of a widow with six children who wished for her compensation money to be paid out because she was 'going to America with her children to enter into a business in which she had had prior experience and she had every reason to believe she could maintain her family there, which she was not able to do in Southampton.' Whatever the truth behind Mrs Wormald's story, you have to admire her sheer gumption and guts at taking her six children on an epic journey across the sea – the same sea that had claimed her husband only months earlier. Maybe the grave visit to Nova Scotia had been a ruse. Did it matter? Perhaps Mrs Wormald did seek a new life, a new start in a very new world. Whatever the truth, I cannot blame her for wanting to leave a city full of impoverished, mourning widows, flooded housing and schools where children often attended without boots, in the hope of giving her children a better life. Who wouldn't?

While tales like Mrs Wormald's brave journey are few, the tales of sorrowful, impoverished widows left behind are many – and the bleak outcomes that became them as a result of their breadwinner's death. One particularly sad story is that of Eleanor, the wife of Arthur Herbert Morgan. They had already lost their two-year-old son Frankie in 1911, a year before Arthur sailed on *Titanic* as a trimmer. But in a further tragic twist, Eleanor was pregnant when her husband went to sea on *Titanic*.

Because on 28 September, five months after her husband had drowned, Eleanor died giving birth to a child.[3] After Eleanor's death, her mother Mrs Earley took her baby grandchild in and was later paid the same allowance her daughter would have got from the Titanic Relief Fund as a widow. Although the baby was an orphan, he was comparatively one of the lucky ones; he had a grandmother to take him in. He would not end up in an orphanage. In another case, that of William Long, a trimmer who died on *Titanic*, two of his five children ended up in a Dr Barnardo's children's home. Money from the Titanic Relief Fund would be made to the children's home from January 1914.[4] His wife received her share of widow's allowance and even his two widowed sisters would receive money from the Fund 'until age 70 or marriage'. But, with two children in a children's home, it appears it was not enough to raise all her children.[5]

Titanic and the widows were, at the start, at the centre of national and international consciousness. The whole world joined in mourning, in memorial services and lamentations. Even a song was released. Today we may be forgiven for thinking that charity records are a modern phenomenon but not so. A charity song entitled 'Be British' by baritone singer Stanley Kirkby was released in 1913 as a memorial to the dead and to raise funds for the families of the victims. It was a strangely languorous jazzy song, extolling the glory and virtues of being British. The lyrics reflected on how the captain and crew saved the women and children first. I wonder what the women and children left behind struggling thought of this record. Perhaps it filled them with pride to have their menfolk's bravery immortalized in song. Or perhaps they were too busy surviving. By early 1913, the Titanic Relief Fund had amassed a total of £418,775 from donations from all over the world. National and local papers had drummed up tremendous support and sympathy, writing of how the 'shadow of starvation must be kept from those who have lost their dear ones,' as the *Daily Mail* put it. Local sub-committees for the relief fund were set up in Southampton, Liverpool, London, Belfast and Exeter. There were rules, though. The allowance paid to a widow would cease if she remarried. The allowance paid to children would cease for males at age 16 and for females at age 18. And finally, no allowance would be given to a dependant (other than a widow) over 70 years old. There would also be deductions if a dependant was in receipt of any permanent income.

Dependants such as mothers, sisters or other relatives also had to prove they really had been dependent on the family member who had died. Like everything at that time, there was a strict class system. The awards given to widows were in tiers according to the job and stipend of the crewman and were listed between Class A at the top and Class G at the bottom. Class A included officers and engineers. Their widows could expect £2 a week and their children 7/6d. Class B covered saloon stewards and bedroom stewards and their widow would receive £1 12s 6d a week and their children 6/3d. Class C covered lower class stewards, catering, boots, bakers and bedroom stewards and their widow would receive £1 6s and the children 5/6d. Class D was for stewards and the widows would receive £1 and the children 3/6d. Class E was for second class stewards, stewardesses and senior firemen. Widows would receive 17/6d and the children 2/6d. Class F was for the greasers whose widows would receive 15/- and their children 2/6d. Finally, at the very bottom, was Class G which covered firemen, scullions and lower-class stewards. These widows would receive 12/6d and their children 2/6d.[6] One of the Class G widows was my great-grandmother Emily. She received 12/6d a week and her children 2/6d until they came of age. Her award, of course, would stop if she remarried. My aunt tells me that until her award came through, Emily continued to take in washing. But once she was given her rightful award, she was able to stop being a launderess for the neighbourhood and focus less on surviving hand to mouth and start to be able to breathe once again. Charles, her eldest, was in work as an errand boy and together with his earnings, the Relief Fund money must have made life ever so slightly easier for the Bessants.

But not everyone was so lucky. For those in the poorer parts of town, they still lived in destitution and poverty despite the enormous national and international kindness. One such case was that of Mrs Barnes who had lost her husband on *Titanic*. As well as her widow's allowance, the Fund found her to be so wanting that they would supply special groceries to her for 12 weeks as she was too poor to buy them. Elsewhere, there are other cases of widows in need urgently of 'nourishing food' as well as their allowance, which shows the poverty they were living in since their husband and breadwinner had died. Another woman whose surname was Clements, a partially dependent sister whose husband had abandoned her and who was letting rooms and doing charring work was given an extension of her award until age 70. Then there was Mrs Cox, a mother of a *Titanic* victim, who was awarded an extra two shillings a week for three months to 'procure extra nourishment owing to extreme weakness caused by severe haemorrhage.'[7]

Then there were the cases of children. One such case is of children Roland and Christopher Biddlecombe. Their father, Reginald Charles Biddlecombe, had worked on *Titanic* as a fireman and had drowned. It seems the boys' mother – and Reginald's wife – had either died or left and the boys were orphaned. They were taken to an orphanage called St Joseph's and their payments from the Relief Fund were made payable to the Mother Superior there. Another, rather strange, case was that of Gladys and May Johnson. Their father, August Johnson, was born in New York and in 1912 he was living in Southampton with his wife and seven children. He boarded *Titanic* as a third-class passenger and died. His wife in Southampton then died and two of his children – referred to as Gladys and May in the Titanic Relief Fund minutes – were placed in a home in Worcester aged 10 and 11 and described as 'feeble minded.'[8] And yet another case was the story of a brother and his two sisters who had a claim entered on their behalf because their brother, aged 20, had died on *Titanic* and they had no other guardian. Before the *Titanic* had sailed, the boy, aged nine, was in a workhouse. After the sinking, the girls were looked after by the Society of Musicians – because their father had been a well-known musician in Southampton – but the boy remained in the workhouse. The minutes about him state a special 'appeal for assistance to assure a thorough education for the boy.'[9]

The result of the *Titanic* sinking was not just a worsening of poverty but of children being made orphans; some left to languish in workhouses or children's homes. As for the women, these wives and mothers were not just *poor* because their husbands had died; some of them were starving and malnourished. Perhaps they gave what food they could to their children, skipping meals themselves. One woman lost eight of her relatives on *Titanic*. All were crew. Her husband, two brothers, son and four cousins all perished. The sense of despair must have seemed unending, waiting for handouts and hoping for a little extra from the Fund to be able to eat. It also seems absurd given the enormous amount in the pot of the Fund. There were millions available by today's standards and yet children were in homes or workhouses and mothers in need of nourishing emergency food deliveries.

But conversely, there are cases where the Fund gave grants for items that, to the reader today, might seem strange. There was Mrs Bishop, mother of Walter Alexander Bishop – who had worked on *Titanic* as a bedroom steward but had died – who was provided with a pair of spectacles from the Fund in 1913. A year later, Mrs Bishop was awarded a compassionate award of £5 to buy a sewing machine.[10] Mrs Carr, mother of Richard Stephen Carr – who had died on *Titanic* working as a trimmer – was given a payment to purchase spectacles too, due to 'being in danger of going totally blind for want of suitable spectacles'.[11] Other cases include women being given awards for sets of false teeth and for visits to the seaside. It seems strange that while some children were in orphanages and other wives were so malnourished they were in need of hand-outs of nourishing food, that the Fund also set aside awards for comparatively nominal requirements such as glasses and false teeth. But why was the award handed out in this piecemeal way? Why were the women not given larger, lump sums to be spent as they needed and wished? Were these women considered so helpless and unable to budget that they could not be trusted with larger amounts of the money that was, by all rights, theirs? Why were some women awarded money for sewing machines while some children of *Titanic* victims were in orphanages? One case was that of William Barnes, a dependant of John Barnes who was a fireman on *Titanic* when he drowned. William suffered from St Vitus Dance – an old term for Sydenham's chorea, a neurological condition which causes sufferers to 'dance' by making rapid, irregular movements. William, then aged nine was living South Stoneham Union, a workhouse. In one of the minutes from the Titanic Relief Fund it appeared that William was in need of payment to re-enter the Union and that the difference should be 'paid from the compassionate fund.'[12] Meanwhile, Mrs Barnes was awarded an extra 2/6d a week for 12 weeks for groceries.[13]

The decisions could, by our twenty-first century standards, appear tough as well. One widow was denied her award from the Fund because their investigations showed that her estranged husband who had died on *Titanic* had not supported her for two years and so she was not eligible. However, they took pity on her child and awarded maintenance payments of 5 shillings a week.[14] There were complicated family set-ups too which made the award system difficult at times. One such case was the dependants of Hugh Walter McElroy who was a purser on *Titanic* and died.

Both his widow and his mother were dependants and during his life McElroy had allowed his mother £240 a year, while his wife had a separate estate. His widow was paying 7/6d per week to her mother-in-law but then remarried which meant McElroy's mother was solely dependent on the Fund. As a result, she was granted 7/6d per week.

Then there was the sad case of Susan Woodford, daughter of Frederick Woodford who died on *Titanic* working as a greaser. His wife died shortly after he did and his daughter Susan was taken in by an aunt, Mrs Pearce, who was granted 2/6d per week which then increased to 5 shillings per week on the Fund.[15] Then there was the payment of £3 16s paid to Robert Scovell's daughter. Scovell had died on *Titanic* working as a second-class steward. Shortly afterwards, his wife died and the Relief Fund awarded his daughter the money for 'funeral expenses'. The sheer range of tragedies which occurred in the aftermath of *Titanic* are hard to fathom. Fathers lost at sea, wives dead, mothers destitute and starving, children made orphans. And all the while a fund with a pot of tens of thousands sitting there and being handed out on a case by case basis.

There were also one-off grants awarded to people in special circumstances. One was that awarded to the widow and dependent son of James Dinenage. The son, aged 20 in 1912, was apprenticed to a carpenter and suffered from consumption and so 'in view of his affliction and small earnings' he was given a special grant of £20 during his apprenticeship.[16] Extra one-off grants were also doled out to widows with sick children, widows who needed extra food and even, in one case, an extra £2 from the compassionate fund to assist in the operation to remove an eye.

But there were other victims, the forgotten ones; the living, walking victims of *Titanic* who did not receive such outcries of public sympathy. The survivors. The focus in the newspapers had, quite rightly, been on the local women and children who now had to survive without their breadwinner. But the crew survivors had endured the biggest shipwreck in history, they had survived clinging to a lifeboat or being hauled into a rescue boat; they'd survived shivering in sub-zero temperatures and watching their ship go down under a perfect, starry, freezing sky. They'd survived hearing their crew mates and passengers – some children – screaming out as they drowned or froze to death in the water. These survivors now came home and sought their sustenance and support too. Crew members returned to Southampton jobless, traumatized and having

Above left: A locket containing the picture of William Edward Bessant. (Doreen Duncan/ Julie Cook)

Above right: Women and children in a street in Chapel, Southampton. (Southampton City Council SeaCity Museum)

The signing-on sheet for *Titanic*. William Edward Bessant's signature can be seen eight rows down from the top. (National Archives)

Relatives queue to view the survivors' list at Canute Road, Southampton. (Southampton City Council SeaCity Museum)

Relatives queue into the night for news of survivors at Canute Road, Southampton. (Southampton City Council SeaCity Museum)

Percy Blake, *Titanic* crew survivor (second from left) in New York. Clothes were donated by locals. (Unknown)

seen the horrors they could not begin to explain. Yet even upon returning to Plymouth, they were not allowed to see their waiting relatives at first because Board of Trade officials needed to get their testimonies about what happened on the night of 15 April. Afterwards, when they reached home, many sought relief from the Fund but in many cases they were turned away. This was recorded in the Titanic Relief Fund minutes regarding the cases of Henry Hogg, Joseph Colgan and H. Baggott: 'The committee are unable to make a grant in case of three survivors who have applied for relief.'[17] These men and others like them had already been held on board the ship *Lapland* at Plymouth for hours while they gave statements. Friends and family had gathered below, trying to catch their eyes through windows but they were kept on board until the process of statement taking was completed. Now, as they came home perhaps hopeful of a slice of the Titanic Relief Fund, they must have been bitterly disappointed. But under the rules, they were not eligible. They could still work. They could still go back to sea. They were not dependants. And so, many survivors – no doubt suffering from post-traumatic stress disorder – did what men did back then; they went back to the sea that had claimed so many of their friends and colleagues. One such man was Harry Yearsley, who had worked on *Titanic* as a saloon steward. He was rescued in a lifeboat and came home. But far from taking time out to get over what must have been the most traumatizing event in his life, Harry simply went back to sea. His son also went to sea when he grew up. As his descendant who I found on social media told me, 'It's what men did back then. They carried on.' Many others went straight back to sea including firemen, stewards, catering staff. Jobs were scarce and there was no hand-out for the men who'd survived if they were still able to work. So it was back to the boats. Some crew survivors were luckier. The crew in lifeboat number one were fortunate enough to share it with Sir Cosmo Duff Gordon, a baronet and Scottish landowner. He gave each crew member, whose pay had stopped as the ship went down, £5 to 'start a new kit'[18] This caused great controversy at the time and it was even suggested that Sir Cosmo had paid the crewmen to row away from the *Titanic* with only 12 people in the lifeboat to save themselves. This was later proved to be unfounded at the British Inquiry. Still, a £5 cheque – just under £400 in today's money – may have at least eased those survivors' worries about how they would eat; for a month or so at least.

Emily Bessant gradually stopped taking in laundry. She didn't know it in 1912 but, in time, she would come up with ideas to help her family out of poverty. She would one day run a sweet shop and even purchase a charabanc (colloquially called a 'sharabang') which her eldest son Charles would drive, taking paying customers on outings. I have no doubt Emily was still bereft and grieving for my great-grandfather. I have no doubt she held it together all day and then wept at night, her poor, cracked, washerwoman's hands slowly healing. But Emily was a woman who wouldn't waste time crying into her tea when the money could be wisely used and invested. That's not to say that her ability to carry on meant that her grief was any less than another widow. It is my belief that, like many other widows who chose to start little businesses, or who announced to the judge presiding over the compensation cases that they wanted to invest their money, that Emily was merely savvy and used to handling William's earnings when he was regularly away at sea. Like so many other wives of seafaring men, this was not a 'little' woman unused to handling the family income. This was a woman whose husband was rarely home to advise or guide her. She was head of her household in William's absence. She had to understand money, saving it, what to spend it on, getting a good bargain. So, there was no point crying now. She had five children to raise and no breadwinner. I believe she made a decision; to use her allotted award money from the Titanic Relief Fund and carry on in William's memory.

Chapter 5

Women: The Good, the 'Bad' and the Delicate

As the bicycle made its way through the streets of Chapel, Southampton, its wheels splashing through puddles, many curtains twitched. Some residents even stepped out of their terraced houses with arms folded to have a peek at this woman they'd never seen before, brazenly cycling down their street. In a world where everyone knew everyone else, where everyone was either a sailor, a ship's fireman, a steward or a seafarer's wife, a newcomer – particularly a well-dressed, female one – stuck out like a sore thumb. Occasionally the bicycle would stop at a house. The smart-looking lady would hop off her cycle, lean it against the wall and knock on the door of the property before being invited inside. Half an hour or so later, she'd re-emerge, wave, climb back on to her bicycle and set off again. This mystery lone female cyclist was soon known by all who met her as The Lady Visitor. She'd been appointed by the powers that be at the Titanic Relief Fund to be the eyes and ears of those in charge of the purse strings. Her name was Ethel Maude Newman and she was in her mid-30s. Her appointment had come after a meeting of the Titanic Relief Fund officials on 28 November 1912. In that meeting, a letter was read from the Public Trustee 'urging the advisability of the appointment of a Lady Visitor forthwith'. This visitor would visit the homes of the *Titanic* victims' dependants and assess if they were getting enough support and that children were being cared for. It was then emphasized at the meeting that 'it would be desirable to appoint a lady professionally trained for such a post; that she should be of good education and social standing, and for choice someone not resident in Southampton.'[1] It must have indeed been an urgent post to fill because just six days later at a meeting on December 4, 1912, the Relief Fund had found their lady. 'After careful consideration,' record the minutes, 'it was resolved that Miss E.M. Newman be appointed to the post at a salary of £100 per annum, plus travelling expenses.'[2] Ten days later, the Committee decided there would now be a need for a sub-committee of ladies only for the purpose of 'conferring from time to time with the Lady Visitor and to consider special points arising upon her report'.[3] Miss Newman had been appointed as a go-between; to look within the family homes, to check behind the closed doors of the *Titanic* widows before reporting back. For the widows, Miss Newman could be the difference between going without food for another week or being assisted and given a week's worth of extra nourishing groceries, or even a compassionate grant for something else you needed, like a pair of glasses or a set of false teeth. Her report was the difference between your child languishing at home with no hope or being sent off on a promising Titanic Relief Fund-funded apprenticeship and a hopeful future. Her opinion and influence mattered and in time she truly helped changed lives.

Her role might have been to visit the homes of those in receipt of charitable hand-outs from the Titanic Relief Fund, but her job was not just to ensure these poor bereaved people were surviving. Her job was also to ensure they were living the right kind of life. That right kind of life meant being sober, taking good care of your children and keeping your house spick and span. We need to remember that in 1912, expectations on women – even lowly working-class women who lived in comparative squalor – were set firmly. Drunkenness, slovenliness and neglect were all serious misdemeanours. And if women were to receive their pay outs from the Relief Fund, they had to behave, or they'd be cut off. It seems strange now to think that women who were rightfully due money because of their husbands' tragic deaths would only continue to receive that money if they behaved in the way society expected. But the Lady Visitor was there to ensure they were doing just that. Her imminent arrival might well have made stomachs churn with anxiety at first – a bit like tidying up frantically before your landlord comes to check your property. One person who was a fatherless child at the time recalled:

> '…father was on the Titanic…was transferred to the Titanic and, of course, he went down…went down when she sank. We had a lady visitor from the Titanic Disaster Fund, she used to come about once a month to see if I was being treated right I suppose.'[4]

It is of course right and proper that children's living standards were checked regularly. Without these checks, many cases of malnourishment, extreme poverty and other problems would have gone un-noted. But one can only imagine the anxiety before a 'Lady Visitor visit' – the frantic cleaning, tidying, perhaps quickly spitting on a hand and smoothing the children's hair into place. On most occasions, the Lady Visitor found no cause for concern and would report back as such. But at other times she found these women wanting in their behaviour and the Fund was duly alerted. One such woman was a Mrs Keegan, about whom the Fund had received an anonymous letter. '…It was stated that a very unsatisfactory condition of things existed in this case' is written in the Titanic Relief Fund minutes. The case was referred to the NSPCC. In another case, it was reported that 'certain facts of an undesirable character' had been reported about a Mrs Foster and her award was suspended pending an inquiry into her daughters' wellbeing. Interestingly it was written that the money for the 'two daughters also stopped unless they can be got into a home.'[5]

Indeed, although most visits showed the Lady Visitor just how hardy and well-intentioned these working-class widows were, doing their best to raise their children on limited budgets while overcoming grief, Miss Newman didn't always find family life to be going well behind closed doors. Mrs Biggs, mother of Edward Charles Biggs who'd perished in his job as a fireman on *Titanic*, had her allowance suspended because she 'had again been before the magistrates on a charge of drunkenness. It was reluctantly decided to suspend her allowance for three months.'[6] She was reinstated three months later but the Fund worried she'd go back to her old ways and trusted her so little that the money would be 'expended for her benefit and not given in cash'.[7] In another case, it was decided that a Mrs Worthman would need to be persuaded to go into a home for inebriates and, if she would not consent, then her already suspended allowance would continue to be suspended.[8]

In our modern society with an improved consideration of helping those in the despair of addiction or substance abuse, it might seem unfeeling that a dependant who'd lost a loved one and a family income was cut off as punishment in this way. But we have to remember how behaviour was viewed in this time – particularly drunkenness. There may well have been pubs in the working-class areas of the city full the brim with hard-drinking firemen and greasers, but woe betide if a woman would drink in the same way, at least publicly. The Lady Visitor's role was not only to ensure that children were being nourished and had boots for school but to also ensure their mothers were behaving as society expected them to. It may have been a new century but this attitude was a hangover from the Victorian expectations and morality pertaining to women; particularly mothers. Queen Victoria had been dead for 11 years by 1912 but her wholesome family values in which she was portrayed as a loving mother and wife still lingered in society. For a woman – a mother – to be found drunk was about as bad a charge and slur on her character as could be imagined.

Of course, drunkenness was expected in the hard-living, hard-drinking slum areas of the city where inebriated ship workers and seamen staggered home from the pub or fought in the streets. Drink must have been one of the few pleasures in a world of harsh, low-paid labour, spells of unemployment, of pawning the family's belongings and regularly having children sick with disease. I have no doubt that some of these women would have allowed themselves the odd nip of Mother's Ruin to keep out the cold and while away the evenings when their husbands were away at sea. But now that these women were in receipt of publicly donated money, their status had changed inexorably. They were no longer simply poor women, previously ignored or sneered at by the upper classes. They were now *Titanic* Widows; they had to live up to their mythical status of bereaved, pure, God-fearing wives and mothers who had lost their dutiful husbands at sea. Nationally and internationally, newspapers wrote of the 'poor widows' and how it was impossible to have any idea of the 'grief and want which hold in their remorseless grasp widows, orphans, parents, families…' and it was observed that these bereaved people would never forget the 'Black Sunday April 14th 1912' for 'so long as their weary lives go on.'[9] These women had been portrayed in the press as saintly, church-going, helpless, desperately poor and bereaved and, now, oh-so-very grateful for the public's sympathy and donations. It didn't look very good to have reports escape to the press that a few of these women were actually splurging the hard-raised money on getting drunk or neglecting their children in favour of the gin bottle. Today, 100 years on, the Lady Visitor's equivalent – social workers and such – might well have to report that a mother was found drunk but there would be steps taken to help and support that woman. Addiction is now rightly seen as an illness. But in 1912, it was simply an enormous shame. If the woman could not stop her ways or enter a 'home for inebriates', the answer was to cut off that woman's allowance. Take away the cash and she'll capitulate and behave. The only trouble was that so often it would be the children too who would suffer. Because of this, cases were frequently reviewed again weeks later to see if the woman in question had improved. In the earlier Mrs Foster's case, six months after she was first cut off for her 'undesirable character', she was reinstated on the Fund and her daughter was sent to a rest home for four weeks.[10] Do as you're told, behave respectably and you'll have your money back, it seemed, was the ethos.

This stern attitude to women who did not behave as they ought to was not simply down to the Lady Visitor or the Titanic Relief Fund. Nationally and internationally, society was worried about women's behaviour. The Suffrage movement was reaching fever pitch and, according to studies at the time, women's drinking and 'intemperance' was also on the increase. The 1896-9 Royal Commission on the Liquor Licensing Laws – completed just 13 years before *Titanic* sank – had concluded that women's drinking was increasing worryingly. One female speaker at the Commission reported on women's secret drinking and drinking at other times than meals was a concern, adding that she had seen this herself 'at restaurants, hotels, railway bars, whilst traveling on trains and staying at country houses.'[11] The powers that be concluded that drunkenness was on the increase among women. So why was this concerning? Firstly, of course, because of the detriment to women's health. In an already diseased, ill strata of society, constantly battling the threat of consumption or diphtheria, the poor did not need alcohol to augment their list of illnesses. But it was also because access to drink – rightly or wrongly – took women away from their status and rightful place as wife and mother in the home. Drink plus women equalled a big threat, particularly at a time of growing women's suffrage. I do not write at all that alcohol would liberate women – far from it – but at this stage in history, alcohol was perceived as something men could enjoy without threatening the social status quo. Whereas if a woman began drinking, all of society with a woman at the heart of the home would surely unravel.

It is because of this that the Relief Fund had to have stern, firmly-drawn views about what made a 'good' woman and a 'bad' one. Aside from the reports of 'drunk' women, many of the excerpts in the Titanic Relief

Fund minute books often refer seemingly casually to women's lifestyle as 'respectable' or 'satisfactory' in her case notes. These remarks may seem throwaway, but they appear often and were important observations – and they were there for a reason; if a woman's lifestyle was satisfactory, she was not a threat and not a 'shame' to society and so was deserving of her award from the Fund. There was the case of Mrs Kerr, a widow, who had remarried but gave birth to a child 'about two months prior to her remarriage'. The circumstances of this case, so the minutes note, would be brought before the next meeting. In another case, Ruth Lee, who was a fully dependent mother, was discussed. Her allowance was extended until she would turn 70 or until marriage but the circumstances of her having 'two illegitimate children' and that her deceased son was also 'an illegitimate son' were brought to bear in her case. Thankfully, the case concluded that despite being a mother of illegitimate children, she led 'a respectable life.'[12] But it is a telling sign of the times that a woman's marital status, her drinking habits, her choice to have or not to have children were all raised when discussing her case. These women *had* to lead the 'right kind' of lives in order to receive their money without having the humiliation of having to wrangle for it.

The inclusion in the minutes of the Relief Fund meetings of women's drinking habits, their maternal ways or lack thereof, their inability to feed themselves nourishing food (and thus, perhaps, an inference at their inability to keep house well), their bringing into the world illegitimate children, their starting relationships with new men after their hero husbands' deaths, meant that these women and their lives were constantly under scrutiny. The sense of fear and anxiety that your award might be suspended or even stopped if you, say, were caught drinking alcohol or happened to form a new relationship which did not end in marriage, must have been ever present. Setting these high standards of behaviour for the women in order to be deserving of their charitable award meant that now these widows and mothers had to not only strive to appear most needy and deserving financially and practically for sums of money or grants for food, but also that they had to appear to be the most deserving *morally.* Is this why some women were given grants for new teeth or trips to the seaside, while others were suspended pending further inquiry because of their unsavoury lifestyles? By setting standards of satisfactory lifestyles for these widows, it became as much about who was the most destitute as who was the most pious and, therefore, the most deserving of charity. Did women have to hide it if they started a new relationship? Probably. Did they have to prepare their house in advance of a visit and tell their children to keep quiet about anything which might jeopardize their receiving future payments from the Fund? I don't doubt it. But this was all added pressure on impoverished women who had already been through so much all their lives. Even before their husbands or sons had died on *Titanic* they had lived in abject poverty, hand to mouth, with ordinary daily life an enormous struggle that the middle and upper classes in charge of the Titanic Relief Fund could not imagine. Their children had often been unable to go to school for lack of boots or because their uniforms were in the pawn shop. In Northam and Chapel, their homes often flooded, ruining everything they owned on the ground floor. They had already been looked down upon by society, living in the roughest, flooded, dirtiest areas of the city, with their husbands fighting other workers for sparse work and doing the lowliest jobs. Now even as they were still recovering from grief, their lives were on display and examined for all to see. Some were deemed respectable and satisfactory, others not. And if your life was not satisfactory the Committee on the Fund had the power to suspend payment until further notice. It is easy to forget that for these women the chance to vote in the nation's politics would be in the distant future. It would not be until 1918 that women over 30 who were also property-owners would be able to vote and a further 10 years on from that in 1928 that ordinary, working class women would be able to vote. Women could also not inherit property on the same terms as men – that would not change until 1918. It follows then that these women, despite being mothers, running families and raising children for so long with no help, were treated in this way when they *were* given help. Emily Bessant is only mentioned in passing in the Titanic Relief Fund minute books. It is only written that her allowance should continue, providing a report on her lifestyle was 'satisfactory'. Since she continued to receive her award, her lifestyle seems to have passed the test of what was deemed acceptable for a widowed mother of five in 1912. There were no references to drunkenness, neglect or other problems. She never remarried, nor did she have any other relationship or fall pregnant again. Emily seems to have quietly, almost invisibly, carried on.

But many other women were struggling, not just financially but emotionally and mentally. It's easy now to look back to the period

100 years ago and focus purely on the financial fall-out of losing a husband who was crew on *Titanic*. The distance of the years between us and them can make it harder to appreciate how these women felt. But these women, however poor, were still as capable of grief and feeling as we are today. Some had only just married. Some had been pregnant only for their husband never to meet the child. Although most news reports focused on the financial implications for these women of losing a breadwinner, soon many reports referred to how the grief would go on long after these women were 'looked after' fiscally. Long after life will have 'subsided to the normal,' wrote the *Leamington Spa Courier*, 'there will still be homes where the breadwinner will be missed, not this year, not next year, but for years to come.'

Because of this growing sense of women's ongoing mental and emotional suffering, some widows and dependants were not only helped financially but were also sent off to respite homes to recuperate. One such rest home was the Dolling Memorial Rest Home for Working Girls, in Worthing, Sussex. The home had been opened in 1903 in memory of the Anglican minister Robert William Radclyffe Dolling. The home offered respite to working women who needed a break and was always appealing to the local notables for donations and gifts which included books and magazines, clothing, plants, children's petticoats, curtains, tables, chairs and armchairs, beds and even a harmonium.[13] Once kitted out with everything it needed – including a pheasant and a turkey at Christmas – the home would take in deserving inmates in need of a rest, if referred by a clergyman, or would take in paying customers. But now the home opened its doors to a new set of exhausted women; the *Titanic* dependants.

Several of the *Titanic* wives and mothers and, in some cases, children were sent there to recuperate after their loss. The Dolling Home may have been a place of respite but there were strict rules for its 'inmates' as the home referred to them. The home was intended to be a 'home of rest for women and girls needing a change of air' and a place where 'hard-worked people may find the holiday they are recommended'. The 'inmates' would need to conform in 'all respects to the Lady Superintendent' and they must all have been recommended by a clergyman or have a subscriber's letter. The inmates had to bring with them a 'change of linen, brush, comb, towels and slippers' and were expected to attend church every Sunday. Any woman bringing alcohol into the home would be required to leave.[14] Sadly, there are no reports or log books from the time of 1912 when the widows or mothers of those lost on *Titanic* were sent to the Dolling Home. But from its rules you can see that it would be a place of rest, yes, but not a place of high larks. Women were expected to behave properly and be respectable according to the norms of the time, attending church each Sunday and abstaining from liquor. But many references are made to *Titanic* widows being sent there for rest and recuperation. For a woman who had lost her husband and only means of financial support; a woman who perhaps for the last several weeks had been taking in washing or worrying at night about how she and her children might survive without an income, the Dolling Home would have been a wonderful break from reality. With its position in Worthing on the sea in West Sussex, the women might well have taken fresh air, walked the promenade and taken some outdoor exercise. After all, the air of Worthing was 'pure and health-giving'.[15]

Worthing had long been a seaside town popular with the Victorians with its pier and esplanade, Punch and Judy shows on the beach, and had even been visited by Queen Victoria and later by Edward VII as well as other royals. To take in proper, health-giving, clean sea air, as opposed to the then perhaps rather more unclean, industrial air of Southampton and its docks, would have been the opportunity of a lifetime for women used to only just surviving. Or it might have been simply an opportunity to rest. One such woman was a Mrs Fielder, the widowed sister of a deceased *Titanic* crewman. She was not only supplied nourishing food from the Relief Fund but was also sent to the Dolling rest home for one month. Vera Foster, the sister of a *Titanic* crewman was also sent there for four weeks. A Mrs Jones was given a compassionate grant from the Fund of £3 to enable her and her child to go the Dolling Home for one month. In fact, if you read through the Relief Fund minutes, you'll find time and again it is written and decided that a widow or other dependant should be 'sent to the Dolling home' on account of needing nourishment or simply a rest. In some cases, children were sent, or mothers and their children together. Referrals were so common that widows and mothers in all probability would have spent time at the Dolling Home at the same time as other widows of the *Titanic* tragedy. They might have already known each by other by sight or been near neighbours. Or they might have only now made acquaintance. They may well have sat together and talked, discussing what jobs their deceased men had done on *Titanic*, how they had died, how each of them had found out about his death. They might have walked the seafront together, or simply discussed strategies on how to keep going now the only breadwinner was gone.

But not every woman who the Fund tried to help survived. Susan Woodford, the wife of Frederick Woodford who had died while working as a greaser on *Titanic*, was told in a letter not long after the tragedy that he had been buried at sea. She was understandably devastated and became seriously ill soon after. Like many widows, she and her eldest daughter were sent to convalescent homes, the first spell being at the Dolling Home in Worthing. But then Susan's daughter Annie Freda died in 1914. The cause was diphtheria, which is referred to often in school log books from the time. A year later, Susan succumbed to 'flu, leaving her other daughter May an orphan. The child was just eight years old. She was taken in by an aunt. It was later discovered that the authorities had made a mistake telling Susan her husband had been buried at sea. His body had actually been found and taken to Canada before being interred in a cemetery in Nova Scotia. But tragically, Susan died never knowing this and even the surviving daughter May never knew there was a grave where her father lay.[16]

Susan Woodford's case was tragic. There are other cases, too, of widows who died of illness not long after their husbands drowned. Perhaps some would have died anyway – illness was rife among the very poor. But for others, one can't help but wonder if the shock and grief of their loss made things a lot worse and brought death all the sooner. For others, though, the chance to go to a convalescent home would have been a one-off opportunity to rest and recuperate after her loss – and these spells in a different location did help. After years of the everyday exhausting work around the house before their husbands died, not to mention the grief and taking in of washing or extra menial work to survive after his death, the Dolling Home, however pious and strict, would have been a chance to simply stop. It was not just the wives and mothers, either. One woman recalled how she was sent there as a young girl after catching ringworm. She recalled how she had to have all her hair cut off and was sent to the home 'because they thought I needed to get over it'.[17]

This provision of a place of rest was a new recognition that even poor people, those often ignored by society, needed time to work through their grief after a tragedy as enormous as *Titanic*. It was also an early recognition that carrying on at the grindstone, washing, cleaning, and acting as if nothing had happened was not the best course of action – even for hardy people such as the poor. It is important to remember that most of these widows, mothers and children, while hoping someday a body might be recovered, would never ever get that thing we now call 'closure' they so needed. While richer people's bodies were recovered and repatriated, poor passengers' bodies and lower crewmembers' bodies were often not. Just after the tragedy, the *Mackay-Bennett*, a small cable repair ship, had been tasked with the horrendous job of recovering bodies from the scene where *Titanic* had foundered in the icy waters of the north Atlantic. But telegrams between the ship and the White Star Line showed that the ship simply could not handle the number of bodies in the water. One telegram detailed the White Star Line urging those on *Mackay-Bennett* that it was 'absolutely essential' that the boat should bring back all the bodies it found. But in a reply, the *Mackay-Bennett* asked would it not be 'better to bury all bodies at sea unless specially requested by relatives to preserve them?'[18] In the end, many first-class passengers were embalmed and taken back to shore for identifying purposes and a proper burial. Many other third-class passengers and crew or those too badly decomposed were buried at sea. Was my great-grandfather's body hauled up onto the boat … and then dropped back down into the water again? Emily would never know. And it was far better that she never would know, if something like that had happened. But it shows how the rule of class affected you as much in death as it did in life. For the poor and the bereaved back in Southampton, there could be no hope of a final goodbye, of a proper burial or funeral service. Even if a body had been found, it would have been interred in Canada and what hope did the average working-class widow in Southampton have of raising the funds to travel there? Bodies of their loved ones – if found at all – were left where they were forever. Their final resting place would always be the sea. And because of this, grieving was made even harder. For these women, struggling to survive but also only ever given the certainty that your husband was 'lost at sea' must have made the process of recovery almost impossible. When the door went, did Emily prick up her ears and feel her heart thud, in case it had been a mistake and William had come home? How could a woman grieve when she had no complete proof her husband was truly dead? Even some descendants I have spoken to have often wondered if 'lost at sea' really meant that in every single case. Some of the descendants I've spoken to have half-joked, half-wondered if in fact their ancestor may have survived and started a new life again in America? There was no way of knowing. It is because of this unending uncertainty and grief that the decision to send some women who were struggling to the respite home was such an important one. Not only did it give them the rest and recuperation they needed; far away from the daily grind and worries about survival, but it also set a precedent for future tragedies for working class people. These people may have been poor, but they still needed the time and space to grieve and recover. Giving them a rest was a declaration that it was not only aristocrats or middle-class people who felt grief. It made poor people feel their sorrow and mental and emotional wellbeing was just as important as that of a richer person or those of more standing in society. Taking these women out of their terraced home where grief, money worries and stress were all too tangible to a rest home to try to recover was more than a simple break to take the sea air. It humanized them.

Of course, despite the Dolling Home's good intentions, it could not keep and feed its inmates forever, however tragic their circumstances. Most *Titanic* dependants were referred for one month only to a convalescent home and then had to return to their ordinary lives in Southampton. I'm certain it cannot have been pleasant to return to the daily chores and hardships of life after having a free comfortable bed, hot nourishing meals provided and walks out on the promenade in the Worthing sea air. Instead of plunging their hands into boiling water in a copper bath to do their washing, for one month, these wives and mothers could simply sit in one of the donated armchairs and think, or talk, or sleep, or just cry. But life went on. Bills needed paying, children had to attend school and somehow these women had to learn to survive without their breadwinners. While the initial burst of international sympathy was huge, it did inevitably begin to die down. As the charity records and charity gala performances dwindled, the *Titanic* widows and mothers had to carry on outside of the spotlight of the world's press. There were still references to the disaster for many years to come and on every anniversary, memorial services were held which sprang the widows and orphans back into the world's collective consciousness. But then more weeks would elapse, and they'd be forgotten once more – a little more as each year passed.

As the months passed, back in Southampton, the Lady Visitor settled into her role and was responsible for ensuring many impoverished women received the financial support they needed. She brought to the attention of the Committee those who were malnourished, those who needed extra money, those who were deserving of a special case grant for new glasses, dental treatment, food parcels. A Mrs Hilda Allsop was given an extra £1 for expenses after her little boy was ill.[19] A year later, in 1914, a Mrs Curtis, a partially dependent mother, was given a grant from the Compassionate Fund for one quart of milk and two eggs daily as well as 3/6d for three months.[20] And a Mrs Charman was granted £2 from the Compassionate Fund in July 1913 to go away after her illness.[21]

When the Lady Visitor was first appointed in her role, it was written in the meeting minutes that her position would take her 'practically all her time'.[22] They had not been joking. From the archive information of all the assistance given to widows and dependants – in all its minute detail, from extra eggs and quarts of milk, to artificial teeth and pairs of glasses, to respite in convalescent homes – it is clear that Miss Newman's head must have swum with the faces, voices, needs and requirements of those she visited and came to know. Her frequent visits must have meant that she might have formed friendships with some of the dependants. If this made things awkward, it didn't seem to affect Miss Newman's ability to perform in her role. By 1919, she was doing such a good job that she had her salary increased to £150 per annum, not a bad wage for the time. Ethel Newman continued to work as the Lady Visitor until 1940, when she died. She had become a friend to many of the *Titanic* crew's widows by then, visiting people monthly or even weekly and seeing them through their sorrows, joys, upheavals. But she had also helped place many fatherless children in apprenticeships they might never have been able to access without the Fund's help.

Emily would have known the Lady Visitor. Her home too would have been checked regularly. On visit days, I imagine her quickly clearing up the front room and plumping a chair for the Lady Visitor to sit on. My aunt Doreen told me that her mother Florence, Emily's daughter, remembered a 'visitor coming every so often'. Perhaps Emily scolded the younger children for bringing dirt into the house on their boots or told them to make themselves scarce during the visit. She didn't receive a bad report and but nor was she seen as struggling enough to be sent to the Dolling Home to recover from her grief. She didn't have to leave her home or seek other lodging. She remained in the family home with her children and made plans. She used some of her award and compensation money to buy a charabanc and asked her eldest son Charles to be the driver. A little business was set up taking paying customers on outings. Grief, however enduring, didn't stop Emily Bessant from trying her utmost to raise her family out of poverty. Her children carried on going to school, to be fed and clothed. I do wonder if she still allowed herself some quiet time at night to reflect on life and her feelings. She had been with William for 20 years. His absence must have been difficult to bear. But if she missed William, her children would never see her cry. As my aunt Doreen told me of Florence's recollections of Emily, 'My mother didn't talk of her crying. She just got on with it. She had to.'

She did indeed. And I can't help but feel a quiet pride at how my great-grandmother seized her charitable hand-outs and compensation, used them as best she could to raise her family and stoically carried on.

Chapter 6

Heroes and 'Cowards'

He dropped his shovel, wiped the sweat that dripped from his soot-covered face and clambered up the listing maze of stairwells with the rest of the Black Gang. When he reached the deck, the shock of the icy air took his breath away. After being down in the boiler room where the heat was unbearable, the night air on deck in the middle of the Atlantic almost froze him to the spot. His mates, their shirts and flannel trousers equally covered in soot and coal, were standing there like skeletons, exhausted from their shift at the furnace and now excitedly gathering near a lifeboat about to be lowered. Many of them were being ordered by officers to help lower lifeboats and to row passengers to safety. 'Come on, Will!' a mate shouted. 'This one's for us!' William was about to rush over and claim his place in the lifeboat, to offer to row with his mates and get off the godforsaken ship that would surely soon be at the bottom of the Atlantic, when he saw him. A rich gentleman looking lost and confused. 'I'll be a moment!' William shouted to his colleagues, before running over to the bewildered aristocrat who was elderly and looking for his family frantically. 'Can I help you, sir?' William asked. 'Let me help you.' And the soot-covered, filthy fireman aided a first-class passenger to another deck, to a waiting lifeboat, to his wife and family – and perhaps safety, if not the chance to say goodbye. When he'd done his good deed, William raced back to his mates and that lifeboat that had his name on it. He bumped into passengers, crew, maids and scullions, all rushing around, lost, some crying, some yelling, some too frozen in the night air to speak or even think. But by the time he made it back to his lifeboat, the group of mates had vanished. The Black Gang was gone. The lifeboat had been lowered and his chance had gone with it. William stood there, his breath making smoke-like clouds in the freezing air and suddenly was able to reflect on his short life. He had spent most of his working life sweating, back and arms aching, shovelling coal into ships'

*furnaces. The rest of his life had been spent worrying about surviving
and how he'd pay another month's rent or about feeding his children.
Now, as life was about to be taken from him, at age only 40, did any of
that matter? What mattered now was this: William would never see his
wife Emily and five children again...*

The above account didn't happen, of course. It's my own fictional,
dramatized make-believe scenario. Or perhaps it did happen, or some
of it did? But it is a story. A story about my great-grandfather that
I believed to be true for many years because it is what my father told
me. Whenever another film or adaptation or documentary was shown
on television about *Titanic*, my father would tell me proudly how his
grandfather and my great-grandfather William Bessant had died helping
another passenger into a lifeboat on *Titanic* and denying himself a place
by being too late. This is the family tale I was told again and again. It
was repeated so often, it became truth; William was a brave man who'd
sacrificed himself saving a richer man. He had not died in vain. He was
not a lowly fireman now. In death, he was saintly. He was good.

The only trouble, I realized as I got older, was there was absolutely
no way of corroborating this story. With the help of another *Titanic*
descendant, Dave Fredericks, whose coal trimmer great-grandfather
Walter Fredericks survived *Titanic*, I know that William was on the
12-4 watch, meaning he worked noon until four pm each day and then
rested eight hours before beginning another shift at 12 midnight until
4 am. As *Titanic* struck the iceberg before midnight, it's guessed that
William would have been preparing for his shift and not yet in the boiler
room. So, was he on his way to a shift or still in his mess, perhaps
dressing? All I knew for certain was that William had died. How he
had died had gone with him to his watery grave. Had William died
because he had helped another passenger to a lifeboat? There was no
way of knowing. There was talk that weeks later after the tragedy, a rich
gentleman had knocked on Emily's door in Southampton, offering to
send her eldest daughter to private school in thanks for William helping
him survive the tragedy but that the child, Gladys, had refused. As a
result, there was no record of any school fees being paid or even who
the rich gentleman was. Again, no proof. Only family pride and stories.
But the myth resounded and became fact, solidifying down the family
generations. Why? Because it was what we all wanted to believe.

In many other families, from passengers to stewards, from kitchen staff to firemen, similar stories were told. In newspaper articles from the time, often women were reported saying proudly that her man had 'done his duty' and died bravely; a hero. But the truth was, no one knew how these people had died and whether there was any 'heroism' or sacrifice involved. But my family – and these families – told themselves these men were heroes because it was a consolation. Believing your loved one had not simply died because he was the lowest member of crew and statistically had no chance of making it but had perished because he had done his duty and saved others in doing so, meant that pride could replace grief. In short, these women needed to create stories and believe their men had been heroes, rather than focus on the terrible unfairness of why their men had died so needlessly. It was the only way they could bear their sorrow.

It wasn't easy, however. Harold Bride, a Marconi wireless operator, afterwards told of how he stayed with John 'Jack' Phillips, the senior wireless officer, sending distress messages until the bitter end, hoping for rescue. During this intensely stressful time, so Bride explained at the Inquiry, a heavily-built stoker entered the Marconi room and tried to steal Phillips's lifebelt. In a statement given at the Inquiry into *Titanic*, Harold Bride told of how a man entered the room and was presumed to be a stoker from his appearance. Bride said that he and Phillips stopped the stoker taking the lifebelt. When asked if he had hit him, Bride replied, 'Well, I held him and Mr Phillips hit him.' Many papers ran the story. The *New York Times* also featured it, along with a cartoon drawing of a rough and burly-looking stoker, complete with broom about his person, attacking the wireless operator and ripping his lifebelt from him. These stories, even if they were true, only added more dark tones to the Black Gang's bad reputation. While their betters, the engineers, and many of their mates were toiling down below in the boiler rooms in the face of death, certain individuals like this particular stoker, were behaving in a cowardly manner and attempting to steal lifejackets which were not theirs. It's no surprise, therefore, that a distant cousin I found whilst researching this book told me that her mother said that our family had said for a long while that William – our shared ancestor – was an 'engineer' and not a fireman, simply because of the intensely negative connotations of being a Black Gang member with all their drinking, fighting and ghastly reputations, especially once the press got hold of the story of a stoker attempting to steal a lifebelt.

The tales of heroism on *Titanic* are legendary and have been immortalised on film and in books. *Titanic* foundered slowly. Because of this slow demise, there was time for people to return to their cabins, to don warm clothes or hats, time in many cases to say heart-wrenching goodbyes, time to be brave or cowardly. Because of this, even though the sinking must have been chaotic and terrifying, many stories of heroism are known and have been recorded. Top Hero of all has to be Benjamin Guggenheim, who famously donned his best evening suit and top hat and said he would not leave like a coward in place of any woman but would die like a gentleman. Colonel John Jacob Astor – the ship's richest passenger – also remained on deck and then lost his life. Press wrote of how 'Jacob Astor, the millionaire' was sitting in a lifeboat with his wife when he saw a woman approach the boat. He 'jumps out and places her by the side of his wife, saying: "I leave her to your charge,"' wrote the *Hastings and St Leonards Observer*. This bravery of the rich and aristocratic, whose deaths surely meant that ordinary third-class women or children could live, made headlines around the world. This heroism of the higher echelons then filtered down to the average, everyday person. For a widow of a crewmember who had died to be able to say 'my husband did as Astor or Guggenheim did' perhaps could have eased her grief somewhat. It would also have elevated her status in society. For the richest and the poorest to all behave 'like gentlemen' meant that by their men's heroism, class could be blurred, albeit for a short time. Heroes were heroes. Whether they were multi-millionaires or humble crew on £6 a month.

The engineers were one group of the crew who were lifted to saintly status. 'Not a single engineer of the *Titanic* was saved,' wrote the *Southern Daily Echo* on April 22, 1912, 'Whilst others were seeking means of escape from a watery grave, the engineering staff were down in the bowels of the ship doing their utmost to keep the vessel afloat.' The following day, the same paper wrote that the engineers had stayed to try to save the ship while in the stokers' case, they had been used to help the seaman get the boats away. Wrote the papers: 'These men, therefore, would have an opportunity to attempt to save themselves when the ship made her final plunge…'

True, the paper acknowledged that the firemen had been ordered by some officers to get away the boats, but was there not a slight sting in the tail of the sentence: 'would have had an opportunity to save themselves...'? Some boiler room staff, such as coal trimmer Walter Fredericks, were employed in rowing the lifeboats to safety. But this inference that some firemen might have used this opportunity to escape while engineers stayed at their posts, is clear. Meanwhile, church services, with the intention of consoling the heartbroken widows and children, helped lift the crew from simply statistics and lists of the dead to immortal hero status. The Bishop of Winchester's sermon which he gave at St Mary's Church, Southampton soon after the tragedy spoke directly to the weeping widows and fatherless children sitting in the pews. He spoke of their men who had drowned in a harangue-like manner. The Bishop said, so the *Southampton Times and Hampshire Express* reported, that:

> 'their last hours in this life were hours of heroic self-sacrifice. Theirs was a noble way to meet death. They would have been ashamed to live if they had secured their life by taking places that might have been filled by the helpless women and children in the vessel.'

This sermon would be more apt after a warriors' battle rather than a tragedy such as the sinking of a ship, but already it showed how the church, the media and, importantly, the women themselves were talking about their menfolk. In another sermon, this time at St Augustine's Church in Northam, the true heart of the community of seafaring families of the *Titanic*, Reverend H.M. Ellis spoke of how the widows would:

> 'be able to teach their children that their fathers died as Christian Englishmen should die; that England would always remember them with thankful pride, and that England was today the better for what they did.' He went on to add that 'the heroic steadfastness with which the crew remained at their posts in order that others might be saved had taught them that they shared a common humanity...'[1]

It is clear that these war-cry, patriotic, rousing sermons must have been a comfort to many of the women and children. Hearing your husband or father be described in this way, after a lifetime of being seen as perhaps the lowliest, soot-stained fireman, must have been akin to being raised to a saintly status in society. But it would not have been so nice to hear if your husband had come safely home. How did women feel – and the male survivors – when the Bishop spoke of how men 'would have been ashamed to live if they had secured their life by taking places that might have been filled by the helpless women and children in the vessel'? This sort of talk was a sort of precursor to the 'white feather' movement which would come a few years later; where women doled out white feathers to men who refused to join the army at the Front in the First World War. If your husband or father died on *Titanic*, he was a hero. You could hold your head high. Whether he was a saint in his living years or whether he was in debt and forever in the pub, the slate was now washed clean. Your dead loved one was a hero. If your husband survived and returned, therefore, what was he? Should he be 'ashamed' that he survived? Should the wives and children? During my research, I've spoken to descendants of men who survived *Titanic* and the prevailing sense seems to be that these men did not advertise the fact they were survivors. Whether this was from a sense of survivors' guilt or simply not wishing to talk about it is unknown. But with sermons such as these, it is hardly surprising that some men perhaps felt it easier and simpler not to tell everyone that they had survived.

The press continued to fuel the fire that men who had drowned had done so saving women's lives. Bruce Ismay, MD of the White Star Line had got himself into a lifeboat and survived. Whereas the designer of the ship, Thomas Andrews, went down with *Titanic*. As a result, Ismay received a thrashing in the press – he was branded a coward because other men had died and he had survived. Sir Cosmo Duff Gordon, who had survived in a lifeboat along with his wife Lucille and her maid Laura Mabel Francatelli, despite being cleared of any bribery for giving cheques for £5 to the oarsmen in his lifeboat, suffered slurs for some time afterwards simply for being a man who survived. In a letter to his siblings, he summed up the feeling perfectly: 'There seems to be a feeling of resentment against any English man being saved.'[2]

This public gladiatorial-style thrashing of big-name survivors such as Ismay or Duff Gordon, and the beatifying of other big-names who perished, such as Captain Smith who died going down with his ship, and designer Thomas Andrews who also died, set a precedent which filtered down the class system all the way to the working class crew who either survived or perished. Surviving, therefore, must have been a bittersweet experience for male crewmembers who made it home. They were alive but at the cost of being made to feel guilty about it.

For the firemen who survived, some were met at first with elated thanks – for they had been told by officers to man the lifeboats and, known for their physical strength and endurance in the boiler rooms of the ship, were told to row the passengers to safety. Theirs had not been the survival of 'cowards', therefore, but the survival of brave men who had helped others escape and live. But for the men who came back who had not rowed lifeboats, returning home to their homes and normal lives must have been a difficult time. With the press destroying good names such as Ismay, while lifting names such as Guggenheim and Astor and Captain Smith to immortal heroes for going down with the ship, simply walking down the street at first must have been something many *Titanic* survivors might have avoided. With the men such as Walter Fredericks who had been on my great-grandfather's watch who had been ordered into a lifeboat and rowed passengers to safety, it must have crossed my great-grandmother's mind as to where on earth William had been at this time. If he'd been on the same watch as Fredericks, had William too been ordered to man a lifeboat? If so, why had he not come home? Or, because he had been due to start a shift, had he been called down to duty in the boiler room – as he was supposed to be between midnight and 4am – and stayed down with the engineers trying desperately to save the ship? Maybe William really had been part of the 'heroic engineers' after all and had been enlisted with trying to keep the ship going until the bitter end? Either way, although Emily had to endure the tremendous grief and financial burden of losing a husband, she could at least nod knowingly to the sermons by those such as the Bishop of Winchester, or could hold her head high as she went into the butcher's shop or the baker's knowing that her Will had not sought a place in a lifeboat in the place of a woman or child but he had died 'as a man should'.

For children, too, the reverence and respect given to their dead fathers might have been of some comfort. Many schools recorded several of their pupils having lost a father or a relative on *Titanic*. These children would now grow up without fathers but now at least they could tell anyone who asked where their father was that he had died a hero. Just two years later, in any case, would their fathers have gone to fight in the First World War if they'd not died on *Titanic*? Many who still had fathers might not have had them within two or three years anyway, given the casualties of the Great War. During their young lives, these children would have no doubt overheard the discussions about work or lack of it between their parents, about money or needing to pawn school clothes and boots so the family could eat. After seeing their fathers' struggles for so long, now they could remember him as an elevated member of society at long last. In death he no longer had to struggle or fight for work at the docks. Religious ministers told church congregations up and down the country of how they encouraged the widows of the *Titanic* crew to tell their children of their fathers' heroism for years to come and 'again and aye again' how men stood on deck while women and children were saved. Of course, initially, seeking consolation in the fact that these men had died heroes detracted from those who really wanted to simply ask why? Rousing sermons of heroism and pride might have stopped many widows and their children asking why on earth this had happened. These fathers, brothers, sons and uncles had died heroically, yes, but why had they? Why were there not enough lifeboats? Why had there not been proper drills to ensure each boat was filled to its capacity? Seeking peace in the fact that churches, the press, and the powerful were now calling these working-class men heroes was one thing. But questions also needed to be asked about why so many had died so needlessly whether it was 'duty' or not.

But why so much emphasis on how a man ought to be? In historical terms we often talk of pre- and post-First World War. But we can also discuss topics such as chivalry, heroism and the suffrage movement as pre- and post-*Titanic* because *Titanic* was more than a tragedy; it was a defining moment in history. Pre-*Titanic*, the suffrage movement and suffragettes were gaining momentum. Women wanted votes and full property ownership rights, but they also wanted equality in their day-to-day treatment. In a world where the threads that bound society were, ever so subtly, starting to unravel, *Titanic*, as horrific as it was, put people in their rightful places again. It put people's minds at ease to see a world where men knew their place and women knew theirs. It was orderly. How it should be.

As *Titanic* sank, some women decided to stay put on board, or refused to leave their husbands. Often these women were cajoled, shouted at or even thrown physically – like mail sacks – into lifeboats by men. The Inquiry, news reports and even church sermons spoke of how many men stood on deck calmly, letting women and children claim places in lifeboats surely knowing they themselves would die. Men who did try to make it into lifeboats were told to get out again, or even threatened. In one recollection of a female survivor, a boy in his teens tried to climb into a lifeboat and, in her testimony, was threatened with a gun and then told to 'be a man' before he dutifully climbed back onto the deck where he waited to die. While these men – and boys – stood on deck about to lose their lives, women were thrust into safety whether it was their choice to climb into a lifeboat or not. That's not to say that women should not be grateful for the enormous heroism men showed in allowing them to live. But it is a sign of the times that, in a world where women were starting to demand more rights with louder and louder voices, that this tragedy should occur in this way and men's heroism be so lauded. Suffragettes may have been shouting about equality, but now in this tragedy men had shown women just how heroic they could be. And a debate ensued. Why should women want the world to change now? After a tragedy as huge as *Titanic*, where men had shown just how wonderful patriarchy could be for women, a system where men perish and women are more likely to live, why on earth would women want the status quo to be any different? Shouldn't this whole suffrage movement just be hushed up now and put to bed?

But early feminists were vocal about their doubts. Lady Aberconway, who founded the Liberal Women's Suffrage Union, wrote in the *Daily Mail* questioning whether 'women and children first' was a true maritime tradition at all and whether it was even a useful one. Many wrote indeed that 'women and children first' had never been written in any maritime law. Debates began in the press with suffragettes arguing that by sacrificing their lives in this way and being heroes or gentlemen, men were infantilising women; taking their choices away from them and, in so doing, denying them their rights. Others, conversely, angrily wrote that women should be grateful for the men's sacrifice so that they might live and that the aftermath of a tragedy of the magnitude of *Titanic* was no time for debate about the suffrage movement. But suffrage and women's rights were a huge part of the debate. Was chivalry a good thing if it kept women in their place in the rest of society? Men and women against the suffrage movement argued that women could not have it both ways – they could not accept men's chivalry in disaster situations such as *Titanic* and then demand rights and the vote later. But it must not be forgotten that among the many hundreds of men who gave their lives for others on *Titanic*, women gave their lives too. While the sermons and news were full of men's heroism, it might have been forgotten by many that there were three female crewmembers on *Titanic* who had also lost their lives. There were 23 female crew in total, made up of stewardesses, a matron and cashiers. Twenty survived but Lucy Violet Snape, Catherine Jane Wallis and Catherine Walsh didn't make it home. Lucy Snape, as already referred to in this book, was a young mother who had recently been widowed. She had a baby daughter, Margaret, who she had left with family while she went to earn money on *Titanic* as a stewardess. Catherine Jane Wallis was also a widow when she signed on as assistant matron and also perished. The third female crewmember to die was Catherine Walsh, a stewardess. Her daughter Kathleen became an orphan after her death and was provided for by the Titanic Relief Fund. Were these women, then, heroines, dying like their male crewmember colleagues? Had they reached the heady heights their male counterparts had for losing their lives? Or were they victims because, under the unwritten rule on *Titanic* of women and children first, ought they not to have been in lifeboats and taken to safety?

The loss of *Titanic* and men's heroic acts in favour of women marked a watershed. If women were to have the vote and equality, surely men's heroism at saving them, perceiving them to be weaker, had set the movement back years, argued early feminists. For the working-class widows, however, the vote must have seemed a distant dream in any case. With their focus firmly on survival rather than suffrage, grasping some small glimmer of pride from the world perceiving their dead husbands as heroes must have been a much-needed boost for the dependants. And it was women too who played their part in making their men into heroes; of perpetuating myths of self-sacrifice and duty and chivalry. Earlier in this book, I refer to the women who, upon finding out their husband had drowned on *Titanic*, were overheard saying how he had 'done his duty' – this statement made even before she had learned how or in which circumstances he had died. This sense that their men had died somehow saving others, or in the place of others, meant that their name would be forever linked with heroism and sacrifice. Just as two years later, it would be women handing out the white feathers to the conscientious objectors, or to men who refused to fight at the Front in the First World War, it was also the *Titanic* widows now who now helped fuel stories of heroism or cowardice; of sacrifice or self-preservation in their own close-knit communities. For many, turning your husband into a hero or saint was a way of enduring grief. It made it easier to bear. Dying 'in vain' is a phrase often used, but in this case, if a husband's death meant that women and children had been saved, then a wife might feel more able to bear her torment at losing him. She would be able to tell others and, more importantly, herself, that her husband had died for a reason and a good cause. Press all over the country sustained this belief. 'These brave men died for women and children,' wrote the *Hastings and St Leonard's Observer*. The reporter encouraged the women to 'carry the new spirit of chivalry into the matter-of-fact world of activities' and that they should 'let them never, by word, gesture, or suggestion lower any woman's self-respect. Let them be ready to lay down their lives for their women, to maintain their integrity, to guard their honour; even by the death of self.' A later passage in the same paper confirmed proudly that the age of chivalry was not dead. Odes, poems and songs were devoted to the heroes who had laid down their lives on *Titanic*. An Augusta Squires wrote a moving poem 'The Black Crew of Titanic, Faithful Until Death', published in the *Leicester Mercury* a month after the disaster, which included lines of how the 'Black Crew' had stayed bravely and fearlessly and asked whether they had thought of their families or wives at home, ending passionately with how they had 'won fame's crown of glory'. It must have been refreshing and wonderful to hear something so positive and complimentary to be written about the Black Gang after so many years of merely being associated with drunkenness, fighting and staggering home covered in soot. Now even the lowliest of crew were elevated to godly status because they had perished. Death equated heroism.

One such man whose slate was wiped clean in death was William Mintram, mentioned earlier in this book. After serving 12 years penal servitude, William then went back to work on the White Star Line ships. His descendant, Quentin Hurst, told me that after William's arrest his children were split up – the girls put into service while three boys were sent to Canada. Family members told Quentin that William had signed on to *Titanic* as a fireman but not just for the work. He had another agenda; he was actually on *Titanic* on the way to Canada in the hope of finding his sons. Along with William Mintram, his son-in-law Walter Hurst was also working as a fireman. Walter was married to William's daughter Rosina. Quentin told me that on the night of the sinking, the two men had between them just one lifebelt. William apparently gave his son-in-law his lifebelt, telling him that he had more use of it. He then drowned and his daughter's husband Walter was saved.

Quentin is Walter's great-grandson and William's great-great-grandson and told me that he believed William Mintram, although having a very rough side to him, was actually rather well-regarded by many and that another side to his story was that the wife William killed used to get drunk in the city centre, smashing windows and was often locked up overnight in cells. Whatever William's past, on *Titanic* he had saved his son-in-law, ensuring his daughter Rosina would get her husband and breadwinner back again. In death, his past was wiped away and he would now be remembered for saving Rosina's husband and dying in his place.

Emily was of course also a fireman's wife. To hear of firemen being spoken about with respect and to have a sense of pride in her husband who previously had been looked down upon by society for his job would have been a new, rather strange feeling. But what if it had been different? What if by some twist of fate William had made it to that lifeboat and had returned, while women and children had died? Would people have shunned the Bessants in the street? Would he have suffered survivor's guilt that his colleagues and other passengers had perished while he was here to tell the tale? Would he have been so shaken by his experience that he might not have been able to go back to work for a time? The prevailing feeling I have got from talking to surviving crew's descendants, is that men didn't talk about the tragedy and hurried back to work on boats as soon as they possibly could. But what if a man was not able to? Indeed, the question of whether crew survivors should also be given relief from the Titanic Relief Fund was also discussed at a meeting in 1912 soon after the relief fund began, but it was concluded that, as only one survivor requiring assistance had come to the notice of the Committee, 'no general recommendation to the Mansion House Committee seemed practicable or desirable'.[3]

Was it a sense of guilt or shame at surviving that meant only one survivor's case had come to the notice of the committee in 1912? Did men simply not want to seek help and put themselves forward? Other men might not have wanted the struggle and wrangle of seeking help and instead decided to go straight back to sea to earn. One descendant of Percy Blake, a trimmer on *Titanic*, told me that at first Percy's family had mistakenly believed him to be dead after his name was wrongly posted on a list of the missing. He later turned up alive but his descendant told me that her mother had no recollection of Percy ever visiting the family or attending family funerals. She said, 'Perhaps he was away at sea most of the time?' Going back to the sea that had claimed so many of their friends and colleagues seemed the bravest thing they could do in a world where survivors, on the whole, felt they could not talk about what they had been through. For those crew who survived who had rowed lifeboats, such as fireman Alfred Charles Shiers, they could hold their heads high in society – as could their wives and families – because they had helped others by lowering lifeboats and rowing them. I found Alfred Shiers's descendant on social media, who told me that he was ordered into a lifeboat by an officer to help row. Walter Fredericks, another fireman who survived, also rowed survivors to safety. Although their descendants could not tell me much about how these men were received by friends or acquaintances back in Southampton, it can be surmised that because they had rowed others to safety, they probably would not have endured some of the negative association other survivors met.

Other crewmembers were racked with shame and guilt, like Quartermaster Robert Hichens, who was at the wheel when *Titanic* struck the iceberg. His descendants told their story to the *Daily Mail* in 2008, of how Hichens was labelled a coward for being in charge of a lifeboat but not rowing back to the foundering *Titanic* to save more passengers. He is the famous character in the epic film *Titanic* who argues with American socialite Molly Brown, when she urges him to go back for more passengers but he refuses. Hichens was, according to his family, racked with guilt for the rest of his life and began drinking heavily. He was even sentenced to five years in prison for attempted murder after shooting someone. His descendant told the newspaper that even some of his own family wanted nothing to do with him. He died in 1940, presumably spending much of life feeling survivors' guilt.

This reaction of press, family, friends and acquaintances must have made life incredibly difficult for survivors in a city such as Southampton; a city where there could be no escape from the disaster. For days, even weeks after the tragedy, curtains in working class homes remained closed in respect. Flags were at half-mast. The docks, the streets, the pubs – all would have talked of nothing but *Titanic* for years to come. In death, the crew who never came home became heroes. If they survived, they had to explain why. One descendant, Lyn Aylett, told me of her grandfather

Albert Haines. Albert was a boatswain's mate who survived *Titanic* and gave evidence at the Inquiry. Lyn told me that the disaster 'just didn't get spoken about' in her family. She said, 'I didn't have one conversation with either my grandmother or father to find out what Albert had told them about that night. I so regret that.' Lyn added that whilst growing up, she felt the *Titanic* story in her family was almost akin to a 'dirty secret'. This is despite Haines helping launch lifeboats and helping row over 50 people to safety. With the dead made into immortal heroes and the survivors left without counselling or support, it's no wonder that most descendants I've spoken to tell me that *Titanic* became a taboo subject rarely spoken about in the families where a crewmember came home – despite how many people they may have helped save.

Even today, in popular representations of *Titanic*, the heroism and stiff upper lip of those who chose not to fight for their own survival but to put women and children first, remain. Some of the most enduring, emotive images and scenes in film representations, certainly for me, are of the husbands and wives saying goodbye – the women being ushered to safety, the men staying to face death. Whether you agree or disagree that this might have set the women's suffrage movement back at a time when it was reaching great momentum, few people can fail to be moved by anyone giving up their life for another, male or female. Is this why *Titanic* is so abiding in our society compared to other tragedies? It surely isn't merely the immense tragedy itself that hooks people's imaginations and inspires such emotive responses, but it's the humanity – the husbands and fathers who must have longed with every fibre of their being to get into a lifeboat but restrained themselves, standing on deck in the freezing cold and accepting it. Likewise, it is the bittersweet sense of sheer relief to be alive that was coupled with shame and guilt that so many male survivors must have felt that appeals to our own innermost empathy and makes the tragedy so enduring. The choices made on board could have been decisions made by any of us. But which choice would we have chosen, we ask ourselves? *Titanic* showed that rich and poor are equally able to be heroic, or self-preserving, selfless or selfish. Class might well have decided how you'd fare statistically but how you chose to act in that situation meant that afterwards you were either labelled hero or 'coward.'

It is for these reasons that I think the story of my great-grandfather saving someone and helping them to a lifeboat has endured and resonated down the years in my family. Whether he did save someone or not is immaterial now. Of course, all my young life I liked to cling to the belief that he did. It was something I too repeated parrot fashion at school, to friends: *My great-granddad died saving another person on* Titanic... Did I have concrete proof? No. What really mattered, I see now, was that this belief gave Emily something to be proud of; a positive story of self-sacrifice to tell others whenever she was offered condolences by friends or neighbours. She, like many other widows, would have fostered these stories of heroism not only to keep the memory of her husband alive, but to ensure the family felt his death was not a complete waste. I can imagine her consoling her own children, then only young. When they asked her where their father was, she could reply that he had died being very brave. The children would then have felt the same sentiment around them in society, at school, at church. In a world where Emily and William and families like them had lived so downtrodden, so hand to mouth for so long, for a hard-working man to die in this way would have been as pathetic as it was painful. Men who had worked so hard, fought for work during strikes and lived in squalid conditions throughout their miserable existence had now died and for what? There would surely have been anger at first. There would also have been questions. Why had he died while another wife's husband had come home? Why should Emily be plunged into destitution and grief and not her neighbour? But anger is tiring; one can only stay angry for so long. It is also time-consuming. These women did not have the time or the means to seek personal justice or hold the powers that be to account. To replace that anger with a fierce pride instead would have made life so much more bearable not only in the initial few months after *Titanic* sank, but for many years to come for Emily and widows like her.

Chapter 7

Mutiny, War and Carrying on

The docks were busy with a flurry of waiting press, crowds of onlookers, baggage handlers and suppliers coming and going. If you were to gaze upwards, though, up on to the decks of the mighty, beautiful ship RMS *Olympic* docked at Southampton, you'd have seen something else. Something strange. Tier after tier of puzzled passenger's faces looked down from the ship. They were staring down at the docks and all asking each other the same thing: Why are we not moving? It was just 10 days after *Titanic* had sunk but already her sister ship *Olympic* was about to set sail from Southampton to New York, carrying 1400 passengers. The world's press still rang out with stories of *Titanic*; tales of amazing survival, tales of horrendous loss, the Inquiry, who was at fault, who was a hero and who was not. But now, back at the docks even so soon after the tragedy, it was business as usual it seemed.

RMS *Olympic* had been the largest ship in the world until *Titanic* arrived. But now that *Titanic* was no more, she was vaulted back to her position as the largest liner on the seas. Like her sister *Titanic*, *Olympic* was a vessel of sheer luxury. The deck plans, fixtures and décor were largely similar to *Titanic* and her ornate staircase arguably as grand. She had sailed into Southampton on 21 April, just six days after the city had heard that *Titanic* was no more. Curtains were still closed in mourning. Streets were still silent in hushed reverence for the dead. Throughout the city, flags were still at half-mast. Yet here she was, about to set sail in all her finery and luxury filled with the rich pleasure-seekers in first class right down to the third-class migrants. It must have been an eerie sight for the people in Southampton. RMS *Olympic* was, arguably, less of a sister ship to *Titanic* and more of an identical twin. Although maritime experts and ship-lovers alike will be able to tell *Olympic* and *Titanic* apart from every minute detail, from a distance and to an untrained eye, the ships were strikingly similar. Both had ornate, neoclassical grand staircases set beneath a light-bathed domed cupola. Both had similar layouts for saloons, promenade decks, smoking rooms and recreation areas. But from a distance, perhaps standing at a point in Southampton and looking down to the docks at this point in 1912, with no photographs to compare, no books listing the two ships' subtle differences, seeing *Olympic*'s four funnels on the skyline must have made those grieving and wondering where their husband, son or brother was gape in awe at the similarity between the two great ships. Indeed, for a city still in shock and mourning, this huge facsimile of a ship on the skyline must have been akin to seeing a very unwelcome ghost. The shape, the funnels, the size. It must have been like seeing *Titanic* back from the dead.

Still, the tragedy that had happened just days earlier had not put off paying customers. She was not empty. As she was due to set sail with 1,400 passengers aboard just 10 days after the horror of *Titanic*, people were clearly still trusting huge liners to get them safely across to America. Like *Titanic*, RMS *Olympic* had not carried enough lifeboats for everyone on board in the past, but this was rectified after the *Titanic* disaster and rushed through in time for her sailing due to take place just days later. But now, as she was due to set sail, as baggage was being unpacked and aristocrats and notables itching to get a drink or a lavish meal in the dining saloon, the passengers were puzzled. Those passengers should have been waving hankies at the watching crowd as *Olympic* set sail for New York. But the passengers were not waving. Nor was the ship moving. Instead, hundreds of faces were staring, dumb-struck, peering over the edges of their decks at the scenes down below on land. Instead of sailing away as crowds cheered, *Olympic* remained stationary in dock. Puzzled members of the crowd on dry land asked each other what on earth was going on. Then, on a gangway at the stern of the ship, a line of serious-looking greasers and fireman who ought to have been toiling in the boiler rooms of the ship, trooped ashore in 'Indian file with their kit bags over their shoulders.'[1] Members of the crowd and waiting press watching blinked, wondering if they were dreaming. But this was no dream. Greasers and firemen were abandoning ship. This, said the powers that be, was mutiny. Their reason for this dramatic display was their – and the passengers' – safety. The firemen were not satisfied with the safety of the collapsible lifeboats on board. Their fears and nerves might, argued some people, have simply been because *Titanic* had only foundered ten days earlier. But the firemen stood their ground. They argued that they would 'not sail in the ship no matter what'. Subsequent random tests were done on the four collapsible boats which showed that, although three were seaworthy, one had a hole in the bottom and was leaking badly. This dispute ended with almost 300 crew leaving the *Olympic* as she was due to sail. But this wasn't all. With crew deserting, the captain began recruiting replacement crew immediately. When the replacement crew began to board ship, more of the original crew began to 'mutiny' – not, this time, because of the unsafe collapsible boats but because they considered the new crew unworthy and inexperienced and so 53 more crewmembers left the ship and these 'mutineers' were taken into custody. There were six quartermasters, one storekeeper and the remaining were greasers and firemen. According to press who witnessed the stand-off, these men offered 'no resistance' to their arrests and were cheerful, chatting and smoking as they were marched away by police.

The 53 mutineers were charged with wilful disobedience and White Star Line brought Captain Clarke of the *Olympic* to testify that the boats were all seaworthy. The verdict went in favour of White Star Line, but the judge decided not to imprison the mutinous crew considering how they must have been unnerved by the *Titanic* disaster just ten days earlier. RMS *Olympic* finally set sail on 15 May 1912. Disobedient and 'mutinous' these men may have been, and passengers were no doubt riled that their trip across the Atlantic was delayed for days. But lowly firemen and other crew were now taking a stand. True, the final part of the mutiny seemed to be more about the crew taking a dislike to the new replacement crew, but many of these men had lost their comrades, men they might have known or worked with before, because of inadequate lifeboats. Men just like them had died just days earlier and now lifeboats (or lifeboat, in this case) were again, they argued, inadequate. They were angry and their voices, silenced up until now, were beginning to be heard. Although these men were no doubt heroes among their fellow strikers, one can imagine the wives of these men and their fears. How would they eat now that their husbands were in custody? They must have been terrified their husbands might now lose the chance of already scant work forever because of their illegal actions and blotting their copy book in this way. But perhaps when weighed up against the very real danger of losing a husband in a similar tragedy to *Titanic* because of inadequate lifeboats, a wife would have backed her husband's strike. The wives who had lost husbands on *Titanic* and the mothers who had lost their sons must have also followed this mutiny case with interest in the press. Many must have felt a sense of pride and camaraderie that men of their dead loved ones' class and rank were taking a stand, if not in their memory at least to raise awareness of the safety of the lifeboats. Although the court had ruled in White Star Line's favour, and although the latter part of the stand-off seemed to be more about a fear from the original crew of working with inexperienced, 'dregs of society' new crewmembers, perhaps – whatever its multi-faceted reasons – this mutiny worked. Because in October 1912, White Star Line suspended *Olympic*'s crossing and withdrew her back to the builders in Belfast. There, the number of lifeboats was increased to be adequate for all passengers aboard and a double, watertight hull was created. This, argued engineers, meant that should RMS *Olympic* ever hit an iceberg in the same way as *Titanic* had been, she would not sink.

Meanwhile, for the *Titanic* widows and children in their terraced homes on dry land, life went on too. Time passed and, as in any era, the widows grieved at different rates. For some, they vowed never to marry again. Others longed for companionship. Perhaps in some cases they had been unhappily married and so now seized the opportunity to find a new man and start again. Four weeks after Christmas, on January 29 1914, the Titanic Relief Fund held their usual meeting. Along with the usual apologies for any absences, discussions of the dependants' lifestyles and how everyone was doing, another list was read out and discussed. It was a list of women for whom their award from the Fund would now be terminated. Not because they'd done anything wrong or were living an unsatisfactory life, but simply because they'd found love again and remarried. Life, it seemed, went on. A Mrs Richards had remarried on 16 December 1913, while a Mrs Slight had married on 23 December. A Mrs Johnston had married on Christmas Day 1913 and Mrs Barringer and Mrs Williams, both widows, had both said their vows to new husbands on 17 January 1914, just 12 days earlier than the date on which this meeting was held. Elsewhere in the minutes from the Relief Fund meetings, it is recorded that the widows who had remarried would receive their final lump sum payment before their award would cease. How much of a lump sum they received depended on their class of award. Almost two years had passed since the disaster and, although many widows remained alone, some of these women were now ready to move on.

Their children were doing the same. Before *Titanic*, many of these children might have had little hope of achieving a great deal after living in such poverty and through such struggle. Boys often left school by age

14, only to follow into their fathers' footsteps and going off on the ships. Girls, on the whole, left school with a few sewing skills to become wives and mothers. But now, the Titanic Relief Fund offered these children who'd lost their fathers a way out; another path. The Fund actively sought to help the fatherless children to continue in their schooling and to find apprenticeships and even helped fund the purchase of equipment needed by young apprentices as well as, in some cases, clothing to attend their courses and jobs. Just two years earlier, these children might have had little hope of affording a place on an apprenticeship or to continue their schooling. In a world where even children's school uniforms or precious school boots ended up temporarily in the pawn shop, hopeful futures were scarce. Not anymore. Even those considered 'cripples' in the unpleasant, archaic term of the early 1900s were given help. One such case was that of a J. Head, who was described in the meeting minutes as 'a cripple' and had previously been boarded out at a 'cripples' college'. The Committee decided that his mother, Mrs Head, a widow, should 'be informed that if she finds some occupation to which he can be apprenticed – say tailoring or boot-making – the Committee would be willing to assist'.[1] A year later, in May 1914, Head was given £10 for an apprenticeship to a bootmakers' as well as a sum 'not exceeding £7 7 shillings and no pence' for a bicycle which was 'to remain property of the Committee'[2] Elsewhere around the city, children were being given opportunities to better themselves. A Muriel Ward was given a £5 grant for an apprenticeship and in 'respect of whom certain fees had been incurred by her mother in having her trained in a business career."[3] And Dorothy Penrose was sent to an evening school and it was suggested that 'a typewriter should be hired'.[4] Meanwhile, Gladys Proctor who wanted to train as a teacher would be given a sum of £20 as an apprenticeship premium.[5] Apprenticeships are discussed frequently in the Titanic Relief Fund books, with hopes to start careers and jobs ranging from hairdressing to engineering, from drapery to chauffeuring and mechanics. Other children were given grants for tools, such as the son whose surname was Smith who received a £10 grant for tools in March 1919.[6] In other cases, children were coached for examinations and apprenticeship grants given for a 'necessary outfit' for going into their line of work. Local firms, who no doubt had been touched by the disaster themselves in some way, came forward to take on the young *Titanic* children into jobs and apprenticeships. In one meeting, the Committee conveyed their thanks to a firm Messrs Thorneycroft for having accepted a boy named Nicholls on as an apprentice at the cost of £30 instead of the usual £50.[7]

The Relief Fund also helped children who wanted to start afresh elsewhere, even abroad. One case was that of widow Mrs Johnson's children. The children, Hubert and Victoria, had been offered a new life in New Zealand by an uncle. The Committee decided that they were prepared to 'make a grant to enable Hubert and Victoria to go to an uncle in New Zealand, who it is understood has undertaken to provide for their future welfare if they can be got out there...'[8] These children and young people, often from the poorest parts of the city, would not have had these opportunities without the help of the Titanic Relief Fund. Their mothers would have no doubt felt a bittersweet pride that on one hand their children would now have far greater opportunities than they could have wished for, but at the huge cost of losing their husband on *Titanic*. The minutes, held in Southampton City Archives, document all these small things going on in people's lives. Many children who are not listed as getting apprenticeships had their school fees paid instead. Many were sent to esteemed local private schools at the expense of the Fund. One descendant I found through social media whose stoker great-grandfather died on *Titanic* told me that her grandmother was sent to a private school after the father died but that it was 'hushed up for some reason'. Perhaps, even though his financial and educational assistance from the Fund was greatly appreciated, it also divided working class people. Now the children who were dependent on a *Titanic* victim were being sent to better schools and elevated thanks to the Fund, while others remained in the same dire situation. But amongst the young people's hopes for the futures, awards ceased because of death too. A daughter of *Titanic* victim Woodford died on 13 August 1914. Mothers of sons died and their awards then of course ended. In many other cases, children simply came of age and their awards ceased as well.

But there were sad cases of children still languishing in children's homes or under the guardianship of people from outside the family. In the case of Mrs Johnson, who died of cancer, her two 'feeble-minded' daughters Gladys and May were in a home in Worcester. The Titanic Relief Fund paid £45 per year for each child to stay in the home. And a dependant whose surname was Morris had their allowance discontinued as they were 'an inmate of the Southampton workhouse'.[9] The daughter of Catherine Walsh Roche, named Kathleen, was only eight when her mother died on *Titanic* was also supported by the Relief Fund. Catherine had signed on to *Titanic* as a stewardess and it seemed her husband was not on the scene. She died in the sinking and her daughter Kathleen was orphaned. The Relief Fund minutes mention her several times with payments going to a Rev. E. Baus, London. Her allowance of 4/6d per week carried on until 1924 when Kathleen would have been 20. During that time, the Committee also authorised school fees and an apprenticeship premium for Kathleen. By 1927, it appeared Kathleen was training for work, as an allowance of £1 monthly would be sent to her from her accumulated allowance until the 'conclusion of her course at the training college'[10] One has to wonder what life would have been like for those who became orphans losing both parents in this way if it were not for the Fund. Yet there still seemed great disparity between those children who were 'lucky' and received grants for education or apprenticeships while others were in workhouses or children's homes.

Emily Bessant continued to receive her class G award. Her five children stayed with her and life carried on. A year after the tragedy, local, national and international papers ran stories of the *Titanic*'s first anniversary. The local paper, the *Southern Daily Echo* ran a whole page packed with personal 'in memoriam' notices – including one from my great-grandmother. The *Daily Echo* wrote mournfully that 'a year ago the world was staggered and Southampton plunged into mourning by the greatest maritime disaster in history'. But left on the upbeat note that it was 'gratifying to know that the material comforts of the dependants of those who died at the post of duty has not been neglected'. Memorials also began to be erected around the city. On 16 April 1913, the local paper reported that a memorial had been unveiled to the musicians on *Titanic*. In time, memorials to the engineers, postal staff, restaurant workers and a fountain in memory of the crew were all unveiled. As the widows and descendants of those who died on *Titanic* tried to settle into their lives with their allotted financial awards and compensation, to make the best of it, putting their children into apprenticeships and through education, something was looming that would surely eclipse *Titanic* – for a time at least. The First World War began in 1914, just two years after *Titanic* foundered. Many local men had died on *Titanic* but now the survivors went off to the Front or joined navy ships to fight in the First World War. Harry Yearsley, a saloon steward who survived *Titanic,* volunteered to fight and served on the ship SS *Braemar Castle*. His descendant who I met through social media searches explained that Harry would have seen no other option than to go back to sea after *Titanic* and would have proudly served his country. Harry's ship served as a troop transport ship and then as a hospital ship before it was blown up when striking a mine while at sea in 1916. Amazingly Harry survived his second near-death experience at sea. But other men were not so lucky. One widow who suffered such losses was Amelia May. Amelia's husband Arthur May had joined *Titanic* as a fireman, like my great-grandfather. His body was never found. She then went on to remarry three years later but her husband William Beecher was killed in the First World War. Amelia then married a third time in 1919.

Did women remarry so soon after their husbands had died on *Titanic* because they had to? Was a woman with children in need of a man in those times to guide her through life? In some cases, probably. Socially at the time, a married woman had greater standing. In other cases, these remarriages happened simply because these communities were tight-knit and tightly packed and a widow with a final lump sum award from the Relief Fund could begin a life again rather comfortably with a new husband. But because the Great War followed so soon after *Titanic*, the city – like many all over Britain – became a kind of waste ground where men were hard to find. First *Titanic* had taken a huge portion of the city's men with her. Then survivors hurried back to sea, emptying the streets further. Then came the war and many men left to fight and died there. Indeed young, marrying-age men were very few in the city and if there were young men around, they likely were suffering from something preventing them from working or going to war, such as consumption or other illness, meaning there was 'something wrong with them'.[11] To find a new, fit, working-age husband in the empty streets of the city would not have just been the desire of many women, it might have been seen as a miracle or great achievement at a time when men were either at sea, dead, or fighting the First World War.

There are far too many horrific tragedies and incidents in the First World War to list in order of horror, but there was one that touched a nerve most for the bereaved families of *Titanic*'s crew. That tragedy was the sinking of the ship the *Lusitania*. With *Titanic* no more, RMS *Lusitania* was for a time the largest ship on earth and had crossed the Atlantic in record time. Like *Titanic*, the *Lusitania* had the most opulent, elegant and luxurious interiors and every modern convenience of the age. And, like *Titanic*, her grandest area was the first-class dining saloon and varied historical styles influenced the décor. She was even renowned for her more comfortable third-class steerage accommodation and more space. On 7 May 1915, RMS *Lusitania* was sailing from New York back to Liverpool. She was 18km from the coast of southern Ireland when a German U-boat torpedoed her. She was a passenger liner and, therefore, ought not to have been a target of war. But it later transpired that *Lusitania* was carrying arms and ammunitions and was, in the eyes of the enemy, a 'legitimate' target. The shock of being struck was so sudden, so intense, that *Lusitania* began to sink instantly. Unlike *Titanic*, which sank slowly, *Lusitania*'s demise was fast. There wasn't, explained the *Southern Daily Echo*, even time to get everyone into the lifeboats – despite, ironically, there being enough lifeboats for every passenger aboard: 'The *Lusitania* went down so rapidly that it was impossible to fill all her boats...' Soon local and national newspapers were reporting on what surely the most unthinkable atrocity by Germany 'the common foe of the human race'.

Despite the crew and male passengers on board adhering to the post-*Titanic* 'chivalrous tradition of the sea' and attempting to put women and children into boats, there simply wasn't time. On *Titanic*, the great and the good had time to don their best evening wear and top hats; to discuss how they would go down like gentlemen. On *Titanic*, there was time for heart-wrenching goodbyes between husbands on deck and their wives torn from their arms and thrown into lifeboats. Not here. *Lusitania* went down in anything between 18 and 20 minutes and newspaper reports at the time reported deaths of 1,396 although later it was learned that 1,191 people died, over 100 of whom were children. If *Titanic* was Southampton's tragedy, then *Lusitania* was Liverpool's and Ireland's. Whereas in *Titanic*'s case many bodies were lost at sea, in the *Lusitania* tragedy, bodies were mostly recovered and then buried in Ireland in mass graves. Many crewmen from Liverpool and Ireland made up the 405 crew who perished. Liverpool had its own docklands communities, just as Southampton did. There was even one Southampton man on board, Charles Thomas Knight, who had signed on as an able seaman. He survived. But many of his crew did not. *Lusitania* was now the tragedy of the day and for the *Titanic* widows and children left behind in Southampton, hearing of her sinking – the sinking of innocent women, children and hardworking crew – sent a chill through their blood. 'There is no town in England, apart, of course, from Liverpool itself which feels greater sympathy with those who are suffering in consequence of the sinking of the *Lusitania* than Southampton,' wrote the *Southern Daily Echo*. Indeed, for the women who had just got themselves on their feet, or the widows who felt ready to remarry and start again, or the children or young people who were starting afresh in apprenticeships, the *Lusitania* disaster was like a punch to the stomach. Suddenly, every old wound was reopened, papers poring over every single detail, the stories of the survivors, the heart-breaking stories of those who were lost. *Titanic* crew wives who were trying desperately to start again would now have read the news about *Lusitania* and they would have been brought back to where they began. It seemed unthinkable that so soon after the greatest maritime disaster in history that this had happened. Was there a curse on any big liner leaving and returning to Britain? The announcement of any new luxurious liner must have made the superstitious among the bereaved families feel that ships and the sea were hexed. Southampton and Liverpool seafarers were almost twinned in their ways of life and culture – both large ports, both providing crew to the most opulent liners of the day. And now the *Titanic* wives could sit at their dinner table, read the newspaper and give a truly sympathetic and heartfelt nod. They understood what the *Lusitania* crewmen's wives were suffering. They grieved for the wives and children of those lost while working on *Lusitania* as only a wife who'd lost her husband in a similar way could.

Ships sinking and atrocities filled the press throughout the Great War. It was a shipping age and, as such, tragedies occurred all too frequently. Yet cursed or not, sons of fathers lost on *Titanic* still went back to sea because it was their livelihood. Far from discouraging them, perhaps these young men went to sea after such tragedies with a sense of pride that they were following in their fathers' footsteps. In schools where several children lost family members, the disaster was commonplace among them in their shared experience and so life carried on. The First World War took many *Titanic* survivors away again to fight, or the sons of *Titanic* victims. The widows and mothers left behind must have had to develop a strong stoical attitude to the risks their menfolk had to take in their work – both, it seems, in peacetime and during wartime. But the First World War and all its horrors began to slowly throw a shadow over the memory of *Titanic*. Yes, over 1,500 had died tragically on the world's then most opulent ship. But now, so had 1,200 innocent passengers and crew on the *Lusitania* as a result of war. Now, news would filter back of not thousands but the tens of thousands losing their lives in the trenches and all the horrors of war. Newspapers of the time are of course patriotic, with little reference to the horrendous experiences we now know soldiers endured in the First World War. But at the time a common enemy found in Germany, especially after the sinking of the *Lusitania*, must have made the remaining bereaved family members all the closer and prouder to be part of that close-knit community of seafaring British folk. Southampton's docks became a hub of activity in the First World War as Britain's 'number one' embarkation port. Troops regularly marched through the city to board naval ships to be taken to the Front. The men who might have become firemen on 'killer ships' like their fathers now donned military uniform and went to serve their country. Factories gave way to producing goods for war and church halls were given over for soldiers to use for recreation or to rest or even write letters home before heading off to war. To see the city's use and purpose changed in this way so suddenly, from that of a commercial port where their menfolk sought work to a military port where their sons would now leave to fight, must have been difficult for the widows and mothers of *Titanic*'s crew. In many cases, a widow's husband had left that very port in 1912 and now her son might well do the same. Worry, doubt, fear and a nagging sense of doom must have been ever present. During the First World War, Southampton port was a flurry of activity, some which ended in victory, some in tragedy. As the war ended in 1918, many women would have lost a second, third or even more family members.

By the tenth anniversary of the loss of *Titanic*, my great-grandmother Emily was 48 years old. Her older children had moved out and married. To mark a decade after *Titanic*'s loss, she and many other widows like her placed memorials in local papers and local papers, in turn, ran many column inches commemorating the sad anniversary. But the tone, although still reverent, had been altered now by the Great War. There had been too much death. Too much sorrow. Too much young blood spilt. The sheer numbers of young lives lost or maimed or injured in the Great War was unfathomable. Still, it was written in the *Southern Daily Echo* that it seemed like Southampton 'will never forget the tragic event ten years ago today which plunged so many of her homes in mourning'. But the immensity of war even in the city synonymous now with *Titanic* qualified that mourning. There was no question, wrote the *Daily Echo*, that the sinking of *Titanic* 'cast a gloom over Trans-Atlantic travel' but added that the horror of that loss of life in 1912 that so touched every street in Southampton was dwarfed now 'by the casualty lists of the world war, compared with which the deaths on board the *Titanic* were but a drop in a bucket...' In 1912 when *Titanic* sank, many wives and mothers received the sympathy of everyone they met on the streets of the city. But now, after four years of horrific war, those same mothers and wives could console each other because by the law of averages, all women would now have lost a husband, a son, a brother, a father. The war gave everybody – *Titanic* crew family member or not – someone to grieve over. And as a result, sympathy both locally and internationally for the families of the crew who died on *Titanic* dwindled. What was 1,500 lost compared to the millions lost in war? A widow could now confide in her neighbour that she still missed and grieved for her husband who died on *Titanic* and the neighbour could then weep on the *Titanic* widow's shoulder of her grief at losing her son in the Great War. The war was a great leveller, leaving no family in the city untouched. Grief became not only the property of the *Titanic* dependants, but that of the entire city and country.

But just as the dependants had had to survive immediately after *Titanic's* loss, so they must now as the country emerged from the war. Savings certificates and bonds that *Titanic* widows had asked to be made ten years earlier now came to maturity. A Nellie Tizard, who it is unclear as to whether was the wife or child dependant of Arthur Tizard who died while working as a fireman on *Titanic*, would in 1926 have 24 national savings certificates realized. These had been bought years earlier in her name by the Lady Visitor Miss Newman.[12] In the Titanic Relief Fund minutes books, the names and tiny domestic details about people's lives now begin to dwindle. Mothers reached pension age or 70 and their awards ceased. Some died. Widows remarried and then were no longer in receipt of the Fund's cash. And children, of course, were now mostly coming of age themselves and no longer mentioned in the Fund's committee meetings. The meeting minutes begin to become eerily silent with far fewer mentions of the domestic life of recipients of awards and compassionate grants.

By 1925, there were 574 dependants still listed on the Titanic Relief Fund. This included 191 widows, 187 children and 196 'others'.[13] As life returned to normal in the 1920s for the *Titanic* crew's families, so did life at the beating heart of the city; its port. Military port no longer, the huge liners of the day now continued to arrive and depart. Ocean travel, although blighted by *Titanic*, *Lusitania* and countless other tragedies during the war, continued to be the luxury choice of transport for the elite, and the only mode of transport for the poor migrating to better lives. On 11 April 1922, almost ten years exactly since *Titanic* had sailed and foundered, a new ship was in town; RMS *Majestic*. This ship had previously been known as the SS *Bismarck* of the Hamburg America Line but was handed over to Britain by Germany in 1920 as reparation for the sinking of HMHS *Britannic*. *Majestic* had been sailing since 1914, but now she would run from Southampton to Cherbourg, to New York, as *Titanic* had done before her. This arrival and this maiden voyage from Southampton would be a tremendous boon and would bring business, trade, passengers to Southampton but would also, importantly, provide work and 'absorb a considerable number of the local unemployed.' It would be necessary,' wrote the *Southern Daily Echo*, to sign on 'several hundred more men and this bring the crew up to about 1000 strong. These men will be signed on at Southampton.' *Titanic* languished, lost, at the bottom of the Atlantic. The victims of *Lusitania* lay buried en masse in Ireland. Thousands of people were grieving both for souls lost on ships or at the Front in France. But now life was moving on again, as it should. Southampton was a great port and great ports carried on. As Emily went about her business and no doubt caught glimpses of the latest luxury liner on the skyline, or read the newspapers extoling the latest liner to arrive in port, she would have nodded sagely. Yes, these boats brought with them wonderful chances for work for the local unemployed men, and Emily would have seen the excitement of younger wives around her as their men found work on ships like the *Majestic*. But she must have always felt the sting of her own bitter memories. She'd have probably recalled her own excitement when William had got a job on *Titanic*; the excited looks on her children's faces, the sense of hope, the promise of more money, more food, a better life. It had been an exciting time full of a positive sense of a better future. But Emily was older now. She was a widow who had lost her husband to the greatest wreck in history. She had lived through great hardship. She knew something else too; that although ships were the lifeblood of her city and many families around her, the sea could give on one hand but always take with the other.

Chapter 8

Changes, Improvements and Acceptance: The Post-*Titanic* Age

It was her son Charles Bessant who reported Emily's death and dealt with the death certificate. It was 1935 and Emily was found at home in the same family house she'd shared with William all those years earlier. The same house where she'd raised their fatherless children after *Titanic* sank. She was 61. The cause of her death was heart failure. Emily died having never remarried or finding a partner again. She died as she had lived, in her little modest home, on a familiar street, having lived an ordinary life but through extraordinary circumstances. There was no fanfare about Emily's life. She was an ordinary, forgettable person. Another *Titanic* widow was ticked off the list of the Titanic Relief Fund recipients, to receive no more money. Emily Bessant was gone and life in Southampton carried on. Liners came and went.

In 1939, the Second World War broke out and the port was once again requisitioned for the military. Southampton was used to war, having endured soldiers marching off to war through its streets. But this war was different. It wasn't 'over there'. It came to us. The Blitz came to Southampton. Houses, churches, factories were all bombed. As police, volunteers and ordinary people on the street cleared rubble, others stood around open-mouthed wondering when this horror would end. In just two nights in 1940, over 700 bombs had been dropped. For the people living there, the docks had once represented the glamorous ocean-liner age of travel and jobs for their husbands and sons. Now the docks were in Hitler's sight as a strategic port. By now, many of the dependants on the Titanic Relief Fund had long come of age, remarried or died of old age. Yet, the meetings still went on as there were still dependants in receipt of their awards or compassionate grants – war or no war. At one such relief fund meeting in September 1942, the case of one Norman Winser was discussed. Norman was the son of Roland Winser who had died on *Titanic* while working as a third-class steward. It seems that Norman, now of working age, had some kind of medical condition which had meant he was still receiving a special grant on the grounds of his inability to earn.[1] However, it came to the Committee's attention that Norman had been working as a police constable while still receiving his grant and had been on duty during the city's heavy air raids through the nights. The Titanic Relief Fund Committee now discussed the fact there had possibly been 'some concealment of his true condition'.[2] On reflection, though, it was then decided to turn a blind eye on this occasion. The Committee heard how Norman had 'regained a sense of confidence in himself' and that he felt he was 'at last a useful member of the community'. As a result, his grant was suspended but no further action was taken. Elsewhere in the Titanic Relief Fund meeting minutes books, there was now far less comment on people's lives, respectability or inability to earn and far more mention of dependants becoming old age pensioners. Thirty years had passed since *Titanic* sank and now there were far fewer homes for the Lady Visitor to check. In fact, according to references in the minutes, she became far more of a companion to the elderly and lonely. Of course, now Miss Newman, the first Lady Visitor, was no more. She died in 1940 and now there was a replacement – a Miss Varah. Things were changing – allowances were increased too, by 5 shillings per week for widows and by 3 shillings a week for other dependants. Occasionally, relatives of survivors of *Titanic*'s crew came forward, like Miss Shiers who was the sister of Alfred Charles Shiers. Alfred had signed on to *Titanic* as a fireman and had survived. Now it was 1946 and he had died and his sister approached the Relief Fund but, after full consideration of the facts the Committee decided that 'no recommendation could be made'.

Other survivors had reached pension age and came forward. Some tried to prove that certain illnesses or medical complaints were *Titanic*-related from 30 years earlier, but they were refused help. One 'survivor dependant' named Simmons had been receiving 12/6d per week and was then found in 1946 to be living at a Home for the Blind. Because he had not notified the home that he was receiving this income and was also receiving 18/- per week in old age pension and health insurance benefits, his allowance from the Titanic Relief Fund was terminated.[3] Another survivor, Charles Edward Judd, asked for help, but the Committee decided that he was not suffering from any disability directly attributable to the *Titanic* disaster and that he had been working for 32 years for the Reading Electricity Company.[4] Other survivors had more luck, such as Albert Pearcey, who had worked on *Titanic* as a pantry steward. In his case, it was decided that advances of £5 should be made to him 'as and when required'.[5] And the case of survivor William Weller, in his 60s in 1946, who had worked on *Titanic* as an able bodied seaman, was discussed. Weller had been working as a temporary night watchman but was not able to work every weekend and was in receipt of money from the Fund. As his rent was unchanged and he was yet to receive his old age pension, the Relief Fund decided that an allowance of 18/- per week should be continued.[6]

By 1947, it was decided that in all cases where widows were receiving allowances from the Fund but were not yet receiving their state pension, their allowance would be increased to 54/- per week from 1 October 1947.[7] But harsh decisions still had to be made such as in the case of widow Mrs Hunt whose survivor husband Albert Sylvanus Hunt had recently died. Albert had worked on *Titanic* as a trimmer and had lost his brother in the sinking. He died in March 1949 and now a month later the same year his widow came to the Fund in search of support. It was decided, though, that no support could be given.[8] Meanwhile, one woman who had been struck off the fund in 1922 came forward again in 1948, some 26 years later. Hilda Allsop had had her allowance suspended in 1922 for her unsatisfactory conduct. Now the Committee requested that this case be investigated with 'view of a compassionate grant being made if a favourable report was received'.[9] She was now 62 and, unusually for the time, Mrs Allsop had seven mortgages. The minutes writer in the Titanic Relief Fund minutes book seemed baffled at this and decided that because of the 'somewhat peculiar circumstances' of Mrs Allsop's case, it would be put forward to the London Executive Committee.

People had died, people had remarried, people had got themselves in financial difficulty. But the aftermath of the effect of *Titanic* on families also became clear now that years had passed. In the case of the Johnson family, whose two 'feeble-minded' daughters had been put into a home in Worcester and where the mother and widow of the husband who'd died on *Titanic* had also died in 1918, the Committee now discovered there was a balance outstanding to the Johnson family who were left. Mrs Johnson had had eight children, 'all underage' when she died. The Relief Fund now noted that the balance of her award had remained undisturbed because the whereabouts of her eight children was unknown.[10] At a subsequent meeting in 1949, it was discovered that one of the daughters, Lily Johnson, had left England to live in Japan and was never heard of again; a son, Philip had drowned, ironically in the Solent in 1929; one daughter had married a carpenter of the home where she had been sent years earlier and others were in New Zealand. An entire family of eight siblings had been blown apart and scattered all over the world after *Titanic*. These children had lost their father on *Titanic*, then their mother had died soon after. Eight siblings had been separated never to see each other again – and they hadn't even been in receipt of the money owed to them.

The aftermath of *Titanic* wasn't just families like the Johnson family split apart, never to see each other again. It was also something survivors lived with – the distress and trauma and, in some cases, the shame of it. I found the descendant of Henry Noss, Cheryl Jensen. She was his granddaughter. Henry had worked as a fireman on *Titanic* and when the evacuation began to take place, he had been ordered into a lifeboat by officers to help row. But Cheryl told me that on his return to Southampton, instead of receiving a hero's welcome for saving lives, Henry Noss was treated as a pariah for surviving and was even called a coward. Henry Noss's shame and pain after the disaster echoed down the years. But it was made far worse by the fact that he had helped get his young nephew, Bertram Noss, a job on *Titanic* too. While Henry had been ordered into a lifeboat and had survived, Bertram had not. Both were firemen but Bertram's body was never found. He was only 21. Cheryl explained to me that Henry never forgave himself for the loss of his nephew and suffered for the rest of his life. She also explained that Henry Noss's wife had endured the terror of thinking her husband was dead when she had seen the name Noss on the list of survivors, but no first name. She had no idea if it was her husband or nephew who had survived. Cheryl told me Mrs Noss had a vision the night before that Harry was safe and the following day a telegram arrived from her husband telling her he was saved. There was elation in the family that Henry had come home but then of course trauma that young Bertram had not. In the years afterwards, so Cheryl told me, local children would tell the family that Henry was a coward. As a result, he never spoke about *Titanic* again. Instead he focused on family life, hand-making wooden toys for his family of 13 children and living a simple life in a three-bed house where his children would top and tail in bed. Despite his pain and guilt, Henry continued to go to sea on ships before working at the docks de-scaling boilers. During the Second World

War, Henry would make soup to sell to the dock workers. His family never asked him about *Titanic* as he could not speak of it again.

These stories come up again and again in the families of survivors. The years passed, a war happened, then a second war, but still these men felt they could not speak of the disaster of that night. They were made to feel guilty, either verbally or simply by a look or an inference that they'd returned and others had not. They carried this guilt with them until they died. This was possibly the case of Frederick Fleet, the lookout who first saw the iceberg on the night *Titanic* sank. Fleet gave evidence at both the U.S Inquiry into *Titanic* and at the British Wreck Commissioner's Inquiry. During his intense interrogations, Fleet gave curt monosyllabic answers in response to how large the iceberg was, how he rang the bell in the crow's nest three times before ringing the quartermaster Hitchens to report the iceberg 'straight ahead.' When asked if he had been provided with any special eyewear to see better from the crow's nest, Fleet said that they had asked for some glasses in Southampton but 'they said there was none for us'.[11] He went on to explain that on the journey from Belfast to Southampton, which he had been on, he had had a pair of glasses but had none from Southampton to New York. When asked if he had had such glasses if he could have seen the iceberg sooner, Fleet replied in his matter-of-fact way that he could have seen it 'sooner enough to get out of the way'.

Fleet returned and carried on living in Southampton. He married and still went to sea for a time, even serving as lookout again, before going from job to job and becoming a street-seller of the local paper, the *Daily Echo*; the same paper that had told the tale of *Titanic* foundering in such detail so many years earlier. In 1965, Frederick Fleet was found hanged. His wife had died and he was evicted from his home. No one knows if his depression was a combination of the loss of his wife, economic difficulties or the grief of *Titanic* he had carried with him all his life. He was given a pauper's burial but years later a headstone was placed on his grave by the Titanic Historical Society. On the centenary of *Titanic,* someone placed a pair of binoculars on his grave as a joke. Distasteful pranks aside, the fact that no one wanted to speak of *Titanic* made it a 'dirty' secret for many years. In fact, so an archivist told me, no one was really interested in the artefacts, Titanic Relief Fund books or other primary sources for several years after the tragedy. Perhaps it was too raw? Too upsetting.

By the 1950s, the dependants on the Relief Fund were dwindling and were now almost all pensioners. One such pensioner was a Mrs Roberts who had emigrated to Canada after the tragedy. She told the Committee that she wanted to return to a nursing home in the UK for the 'remainder of her life'. But the Committee ruled that there were too many on waiting lists for homes in the UK and that, given her age of 77, it would be 'unwise' to make the journey to Britain.[12] By 1957, the Committee began to think about winding down the Fund and were requested to consider the 'question of purchasing annuities for the remaining dependants of the *Titanic* fund'.[13] But at later meetings, this decision was proven difficult to take. Some feared that the services of the Lady Visitor, now the third Lady Visitor, a Mrs Fall, still visiting the elderly and infirm *Titanic* dependants, would be lost. There were 12 dependants, recorded one meeting of the Committee, who 'through circumstances of health, the services of the Lady Visitor were essential'. There were also, it seemed 17 dependants who needed the Lady Visitor to give them their monthly allowances in cash as they were too infirm to cash cheques.[14] By 1958, though, a decision had been made and annuities were purchased for all the dependants remaining and would be paid monthly. There was some £1,500 left over, which was set aside for future compassionate relief and the Lady Visitor would be kept on for visits for those who needed her as quite a few were 'bedridden or confined to their houses'.[15] Emily Bessant's name is absent from the third and final relief book because she had died in 1935. Her children all married or found work and so the Bessant name no longer appeared in receipt of awards. Had she lived longer, she too might have been a house-bound pensioner receiving much-appreciated visits from the Lady Visitor. For many of the elderly, it might have been a friendly face and something to look forward to. But it might also have been a continuous reminder of the tragedy of so many years earlier. The final Titanic Relief Fund meeting listed in the minutes book took place on 5 January 1959 at 3pm. They confirmed that the amount set aside for the Southampton area by way of compassionate relief would be £1,500. The Lady Visitor, it was decided, would be kept on in her role until 31 March 1959.[16] The Committee said that they wished to 'convey their thanks to the Lady Visitor for the services she had rendered to the Fund.' They also praised her 'kind and sympathetic interest in the welfare of the dependants.'[17]

During the 1950s, and in the years that followed the final meeting, many of the final dependants died. *Titanic* continued to be something, on the whole, that remaining descendants did not talk about. Although memorials were now dotted around the city and although the local newspapers continued to acknowledge the disaster every April, in the early Fifties, *Titanic* was not yet the international tragedy we think of it as today. Many grown up children of *Titanic* survivors knew not to talk about it. Many who had lost their fathers either barely knew them or had lived for years with their grief. It wasn't, arguably, until Walter Lord wrote the bestseller *A Night to Remember* that *Titanic* became the tragedy we know it as now. In 1958, the film of the same name based on Lord's book followed, bringing all the drama and suspense of the tragedy to the big screen. It was a huge success, just as the book had been and *Titanic* from then on began to be something in the world's collective thoughts. It wasn't simply a great tragedy now. It was a *story*. As people's attitudes to class began to change, as people became slowly more socially mobile, *Titanic* became an icon of an age quite literally frozen in time. This was an age people could now look back at with either distaste at the huge difference between rich and poor (and as a result the chances of surviving such a tragedy based on your class) or, conversely, others began to look back at *Titanic* with a rose-tinted fondness. It was a fondness for an age that would never come again; where the rich knew their place and the poor knew theirs. *Titanic* encapsulated all these emotions and layers of society all on board one beautiful ship. Book after book followed. *Titanic* was picked apart from biographies of the rich and famous on board, to biographies of survivors such as nurse Violet Jessop who survived. Many began asking why it had happened and conspiracy theories began to spread. *Titanic* was now no longer the biggest tragedy of the seas, she was the most *popular story*. Was it because 40 years had passed by the 1950s that the story could begin to be told in this way? Tragedies are often too raw, too 'new' to be spoken of or dramatized when time has not yet passed. But as years, then decades elapse, a tragedy becomes less raw and more acceptable to discuss, write about or dramatize.

For me, the *Titanic* story had always been in my family. But at the impressionable age of 20 I went to the cinema to see James Cameron's epic *Titanic* and was left both astounded and emotionally drained. For me, it was the beginning of understanding that the *Titanic* story was not just something my father talked about every so often, lamenting how our poor ancestor William had died and how Emily had struggled. I realized after watching the film that *Titanic* was not *our* story at all.

It belonged to the world. Fanatics, ship-lovers, conspiracy theorists, history lovers – *Titanic* appeals to all and on so many levels. It is therefore not simply the tragedy, but it is the way the tragedy is told. The fact that *Titanic* foundered so slowly means that we have the memories, testimonies and statements of those who saw the tragedy happen around them: the wives torn from their husbands' arms; the babies thrown into lifeboats; the stoical men standing on deck knowing they faced death. It must have been hard for the few survivors or dependants who lived through the Fifties as media representations of *Titanic* began to emerge turning their tragedy into a piece of cinema or a bestselling book. But *Titanic* grew and grew in popularity and became the stuff of legend. When the wreck was found in 1985, *Titanic* fever struck the world again. She was there, lying at the bottom of the ocean but she had been found. Many of her chandeliers were said to be still hanging, much of the shape of her interior was still recognisable. Suddenly *Titanic* was not only a myth or legend, she could be found and seen, one day perhaps even touched. The word iceberg became synonymous with *Titanic*. Ditto the phrase 'sinking ship'. As years passed, as well as moving and sad representations, comedians would joke about it and parodies and sketches would be performed about it. The distance of time made *Titanic* something anyone could talk about, joke about or dramatize without feeling they were offending anyone. But they were offending some people. My father, for one, hated anyone making light of it. John Edward Puzey's descendant Mike Knowlton also told me that his family felt the same and that a relative would turn off the television if anyone made a joke about the disaster.

But *Titanic* didn't just have an enormous impact on the arts, and on cinema and culture. The tragedy also would cast a shadow over sea travel forever but there would be good to come out of it – RMS *Olympic* ensured there were enough lifeboats on board in the year after her sister ship went down. Lowly firemen risked being jailed for mutiny on *Olympic* and took a stand, refusing to sail unless a boat had the necessary safety checks. In the Atlantic, iceberg patrols became stricter and happened more often, lifeboat drills became mandatory and, biggest of all was that 1914 saw the International Convention for the Safety of Life at Sea. Calls had come for such a standardisation of safety from soon after *Titanic* had sunk. 'A greater reduction in speed in fog and ice,' was announced by the hastily-convened Committee of

Survivors who had put together a statement for the world's waiting press whilst on board their rescue ship *Carpathia*. 'In conclusion,' so said the Committee of Survivors, 'we suggest that an international conference should be called, and we recommend the passage of identical laws providing for the safety of all at sea.'[18] Not long after, this happened. SOLAS – The International Convention for the Safety of Life at Sea – was formed in direct response to the *Titanic* sinking. It was a wake-up call – that the patchy, irregular standards of safety that varied from ship to ship, from ocean to ocean needed to be standardized. The minutes of the convention meetings list everything in minute detail from the size lifeboats should now be, to how many people a lifeboat should carry depending on their age and size, how strong the davits had to be to lower the vessels safely and quickly into the water, from equipment needed from oars to lanterns.[19] The Safety of Life at Sea convention was then published, which in its preamble recognized that there was a 'desirability of determining by common agreement certain uniform rules with respect to the safety of life at sea'.[20] One of first items to be recorded is that of speed around suspected ice and that when ice was reported around any ship, the master was bound to proceed at a moderate speed or alter the course.[21] Tragic accidents would of course still happen. But at least post-*Titanic*, there were common rules and standards in place.

As time passed, another form of transport became ever more popular; air travel. This form of transport began as something for the rich elite only. In the 1950s, airlines began to promote commercial flights as the new way to travel. Passengers were impeccably dressed, advertisements featured impossibly glamorous air stewardesses, full meals were provided and – something most of us long for today – there was a luxurious amount of leg room. Air travel began to be seen as the height of fashion and the ocean liners seemed a bit dated in comparison. At first, prices meant only the richest could travel. It wasn't only fashionable. It was convenient. Why would you travel for days at sea when you could reach your destination in just a few hours? Gradually, as air travel became more affordable in the 1960s and 1970s, ocean liners seemed even more of a method of transport from the past; a golden age of slow travel. Technology had moved on now. Air travel was the 'jet-set' way to go. These travel changes and preferences too helped the *Titanic* disaster seem even more distant and of the past a different era entirely. As a result, it meant that it became easier and easier to talk about *Titanic* without shame or apology. And in Southampton, as the years passed the feeling about *Titanic* began to change too.

It was subtle at first, almost unnoticed. Southampton had lived through two world wars and focus on its famous lost ship was still there but not at the forefront. But as the years passed, things did change. *Titanic* gradually became something the city could commemorate rather than hush up or hope to forget. As the dependants and survivors died and their grief and guilt along with them, people of the city were able to view the tragedy from a different angle, a more detached angle. *Titanic* belonged to the world now but the tragedy and many of the memories and the people – didn't they surely belong to Southampton? People began to enter into dialogue about *Titanic*; a topic that had always been spoken about either with hushed reverence or even shame. But wasn't the *Titanic* something the city should be proud of rather than try to sanitise and gloss over? Shouldn't we try to remember and commemorate what the city's workers did and how they sacrificed themselves on board? Work began. Thanks to the work of tireless local historians, such as the late Brian Ticehurst who worked endlessly to source the backgrounds of each and every crewmember, the people who made up the crew of *Titanic* began to be remembered at last. Names crept out into the open. Biographies were put together in pamphlets and in local libraries – this time not of rich aristocrats from *Titanic* that the world knew well, but biographies of humble ordinary people from the poorest parts of the city. Lists were made and published. Names were added to graves. In 2012, to mark the centenary, Southampton's SeaCity museum was opened which holds a permanent *Titanic* exhibition. Tourists began to come to the city, not just as a stopping off point on a cruise ship, but to see the city from where *Titanic* sailed, to visit the museum and get a sense of the city that suffered so greatly after her loss. Slowly, *Titanic* became something the city could shout about proudly rather than a selection of closed doors where collective family secrets had to be brushed aside.

Yet for families who carried on living with the tragedy, the story has been different. Many descendants of *Titanic* survivors and victims alike have told me of their families 'hushing up' everything, from a lucky dependent child being sent to a private school by the Titanic Relief Fund, to men feeling unable to admit their shame and guilt at surviving. Lyn Aylett, a descendant of survivor Albert Haines, told me of her sadness at how her family almost covered up their family history of the tragedy, saying that she didn't even think to ask where her great-grandfather was buried. Still, a few years later she managed to find his grave and was touched to see that his connection to *Titanic* had been marked. Albert Haines, who rowed passengers to safety, died by being hit by a car in 1933. His family spent all his life and much of their own lives never talking about *Titanic*.

Linda Gregory, descendant of Alfred Geer, a stoker who died on *Titanic*, said that her remaining relatives had always avoided talking of Alfred's death. But she went to a cemetery in Southampton on the centenary and managed to find the graves of Alfred's parents and found that Alfred's name was added to their grave, despite his body never being found. Two American journalists who were reporting on the centenary took photos of the family members laying flowers in Alfred's memory; the emotion and sadness of *Titanic* resounded around the world. The city commemorated the centenary solemnly. Descendants gathered at the dockside and threw flowers into the water. A minute's silence was held. A recording of *Titanic*'s whistle was even played out at midday – 100 years to the minute that she left Southampton docks. Even a century on, many wept or blinked away tears. A hundred years separates the city from the tragedy and yet, when remembered and remembered deeply, it is as raw as it ever was. A generation of Southampton families was erased when *Titanic* sank. Hundreds of children never saw their father again. Hundreds of widows never saw their husband again. Mothers who had waved off young, fresh-faced sons hopeful only of earning some money wept over their child who had died decades too soon. Entire communities, such as the close-knit seafaring areas of Northam and Chapel were decimated by *Titanic*'s loss. Streets lost several men. Neighbours lost close friends. Schools all had several pupils who put their hands in their air, their little faces numb with shock when they were asked, 'Who here has lost someone on *Titanic*?' It's difficult to express how keenly the city felt the disaster. It ended the happiness and family units of literally hundreds of people. In cases like the Johnson family, children were split apart, sent to different cities, different countries even, never to see each other again. The Titanic Relief Fund was a godsend and there is no doubt it kept many families alive, especially during the early days after the breadwinner died. I know myself first hand that my great-grandmother raised her children with the Relief Fund award given to her. Without it, who knows what would have happened to my own family? But so much needless guilt and shame was felt by survivors who, by today's standards, would be received as heroes for rowing passengers to safety, not cowards for having lived at all. So much needless poverty was endured both before and after *Titanic* foundered. So many families were made to shudder or change the subject or walk away if the word '*Titanic*' was ever mentioned.

We now talk about stages of grief when grieving over a loved one. The relatives affected by *Titanic* – and arguably the whole world who feels touched by the tragedy – have gone through many stages of their own 'grief' over the last 100 years. First, shock. The world's initial stunned awe at the world's biggest superliner of the day foundering. She was unsinkable. It was therefore disbelief that was the world's first stage of grief. Next came pain. The widows who collapsed when hearing their loved one was dead. The women who fainted in the dock when having to give evidence at compensation hearings simply to get money to survive; money that was by rights theirs. The next world stage of grief was anger. Why did this have to happen? Firemen walked off *Olympic* in mutiny at the lifeboats being insufficiently safe. The poor began to question the value of their own lives as workers. Next came reflection – could the families carry on? Wives who had nothing, women who had only just married or had a baby, sought to reflect on their loss, going to the Dolling Home in Worthing, resting, talking to each other. Finally came acceptance. But with that, finally, came a sense of hope. *Titanic* meant that the world's seafaring safety conventions changed. From that alone, many lives must surely have been saved. *Titanic* meant that never again would there not be enough lifeboats for every single person – man, woman, child, passenger or crewmember – to have their chance to survive. But every ship that foundered or sank since would be compared to *Titanic*. None more so than the fate of the Italian ship *Costa Concordia*, which sank in 2012 near to the Island of Giglio, off the coast of Tuscany. Its fate was immediately compared widely in the media with that of *Titanic*. *Costa Concordia* began listing after she hit a rock off Giglio Island. The investigation into the tragedy, in which 32 passengers lost their lives, was that the ship was sailing too close to the coast in a poorly lit area, at an unsafe distance at night and at a high speed. Newspapers around the world compared the two tragedies, which happened, ironically, 100 years apart. Images of the two vessels were placed side by side – *Titanic* with her bow going down and stern going up and *Concordia* lying on her side. The eerie comparisons were felt even more because the tragedy happened at night, in the dark with the lights on board twinkling. Although the loss of life was significantly smaller, comparisons were made. It was also clear that even though 100 years had passed, and safety was now standardized, we had better communication methods now, faster rescue services, terrible accidents could still happen at sea. The message many people seemed to get from this was that *Titanic could* happen again – albeit on a different scale, in a different place. Despite improvements in technology, safety, rescue drills, man was not above the sea.

Titanic also meant that women and men debated chivalry and heroism and women's rights during the fever pitch of the women's suffrage movement. One hundred years on and looking back, it's clear to see that *Titanic* helped fuel that debate. Women were saved in place of men. Some women asked if it was right that men sacrificed themselves for women and what effect this would have on women's rights. There was anger at first. Many felt women who questioned this unwritten law of the sea of women and children first were being ungrateful and using a great tragedy to simply fuel debate. But then men too began to realise after *Titanic* and after the First World War that they were not – and should not be considered as – disposable cannon-fodder because of their sex and class. Things changed for the better after *Titanic* and now, having met dozens of descendants of *Titanic* victims and survivors, I know first-hand that we are at the final stage of hope. It is resonant here in *Titanic*'s city but also in every memory these people have of their family members. The aftermath of *Titanic* is and always will be a sense of profound sadness and great loss and of a tragedy that was ultimately preventable. But that terrible loss led to immense changes the world over; from safety at sea to views on the class system which we now have to see through hopeful eyes. This is what has happened in the post-*Titanic* age. So, when presented with all this positive change and as a direct descendant of a victim of *Titanic*, I can vouch for the fact although I will always see my great-grandfather's death as tragic, it really was not in vain.

Chapter 9

Lost Voices

The area around Southampton docks, where children once played under reams of hanging laundry, where women with arms red-raw from doing the washing by hand stood proudly on their front door steps, and where coal-streaked dock and ship workers staggered home from their shifts has now almost vanished. In its place tall, smart tower blocks of modern apartments are being built. There's a vibrant student life. It is trendy. Up-and-coming. So very … *clean.* Instead of seeing exhausted 'skeleton' firemen returning home, their kit bags over their shoulders, we now only see smartly-dressed tourists emerging from the docks where their mega-ship has docked en route to somewhere else, somewhere more glamorous and exotic. Apron-wearing mothers and wives no longer stand on their front door steps, waiting for their husbands to return from the 'killer' ships. Henry Road, where my great-grandmother raised her five children after William died, is a quiet residential street. Some of the terraced houses remain but newer ones are there too now with double glazed windows and smart cars outside. In the course of writing this book, I walked down that road and lingered outside the house where William would have left from to board RMS *Titanic*. I stood by the same house where Emily and he raised five children, where they laughed, ate, argued, worried and survived together; that same house where Emily would receive the news days later that William was lost at sea and would not be coming home. I paused and closed my eyes, trying to ignore the din of traffic not too far away in central Southampton; the sound of far-off trains whizzing past. I tried to feel, to sense my great-grandparents and their lives. Emily hurrying the children to school, Emily talking to friends in the street, Emily – in the weeks after *Titanic* foundered – rushing to her front door every time she heard a noise in case it was him; in case there had been a dreadful error and it was William coming home. A photograph my aunt showed me, which was taken around five years after the *Titanic* disaster, helped me feel closer to my great-grandmother. In it, Emily, then only in her early 40s, sits in a black dress, her four children standing around her. Charles, her eldest, is absent – working perhaps or in the army. Another figure is, of course, notably absent too. But look carefully at the picture and William is with her and the children in a gold locket containing his photograph hanging around Emily's neck. Did she wear that locket to include William in the family photograph? I like to think she did. In the course of researching this book, I've visited the SeaCity museum in Southampton, walked around their *Titanic* exhibition dozens of times, walked to the docks and to Canute Road, where my great-grandfather signed on to RMS *Titanic* and where women and children waited just a few days later to see if their loved one was one of the dead. I've walked the path of crew and their wives, imagining Southampton as it was 100 years ago and trying to sense how my great-grandmother felt when the man she'd married and had children with vanished forever under the waves, somewhere cold and dark and so many miles away. Southampton's lifeblood is ships. It still lives and breathes big cruise liners but in a different way now, a high-tech, glossy, sanitised way. I live in the suburbs, away from the docks but on a foggy day I can still hear the plaintive sound of the ships' horns through the mist. Boats, ships, sailing – they are all in all our blood who live here, whether we are connected directly to *Titanic* or not.

But why *Titanic* in particular? Why is the memory of this tragedy so enduring? Since *Titanic* sank, there have been a multitude of national and international tragedies of far greater proportion than hers and with an infinitely greater number of lost lives. Millions of people died in the First World War, and millions more in the Second World War. The 9/11 attacks killed almost 3000 and terrorism globally has killed tens of thousands. What is it about the tragedy of *Titanic* where 1,500 people died that compels us the way it does? Why is its myth so enduring? I've spoken to people from all walks of life in a bid to try and understand. Some said it's the glamour of the ship that lures us and keeps *Titanic* ever present in our minds; that the famous names on board and their collective wealth cannot help but add to her allure. According to reports at the time of the sinking, the wealth of the richest onboard was £120 million. J.J. Astor was, according to reports, worth £30 million. Benjamin Guggenheim's fortune was said to be £20 million. The world's most powerful men were aboard *Titanic* – 'great merchants, the princes of trade, the controller of the world's markets.'[1] The idea that such powerful men who controlled the world could suddenly lose their lives in this way is compelling. Others I have asked said *Titanic*'s appeal comes not from the rich, but from the fact that although *Titanic* represented everything negative about the class system that when it came to the moment of impact, all classes were thrown together in their need to survive. If *Titanic* was man's hubris, the iceberg it struck that night was the great leveller. For some it is simply the fact that the world's largest and most opulent ship could become so very helpless, like a toy dashed against that iceberg by an angry Greek god who wanted to teach us all a lesson. I spoke to David Scott-Beddard, Honorary Secretary of the British Titanic Society, who said that the disaster has captured the public's imagination for decades, 'virtually from the time of the sinking.' He added that the fact *Titanic* was the world's biggest and grandest ship with some of the richest and most famous names of the period on board, it has 'all the elements needed for a blockbuster'. He also reminded me that the story of *Titanic* is still part of our National Curriculum in the UK. 'Every school pupil will hear of the tragedy in their history lessons,' he told me, 'guaranteeing her place as the "second greatest story ever told".' It certainly is a story everyone seems to know. I am still not sure what keeps everyone talking about *Titanic*. Ask any person from any country about it, and they will know the ship's name. Mention the word 'iceberg' in any context, and immediately *Titanic* springs to mind. See any young people on a cruise or even a small boat and you'll find endless jokey pictures they take of themselves 'doing a Rose and Jack' at the ship's bow. *Titanic* has become a part of all of us; a modern day myth or legend. And its story is universal. One can argue you can 'pick' the element of the tragedy that appeals the most – love, death, sacrifice, bravery; choose the *Titanic* story that strikes a chord in you.

As the years since *Titanic*'s loss have passed, the world now talks not of the wreck but of memorabilia. The violin that was played by *Titanic* musician Wallace Hartley sold at auction in 2013 for £900,000. A plan of the ship used at the 1912 inquiry into the sinking sold for £220,000 in 2011. Over the years, items as varied as pocket watches to menus and even biscuits have sold for incredible prices at auction for collectors. Why do these collectors want these pieces? Because they long to own a piece of *Titanic*; a piece of history. To some it might seem distasteful and indeed some relatives have been vocal in the press over the years that the buying and selling of *Titanic* victims' belongings is akin to grave-robbing. But it doesn't stop the prices rising. Distasteful or not, people long to own and hold a piece of history from *Titanic* because it represents an era that went down with the ship. This sense of *Titanic* items and memories being for sale only increases my sadness for those who perished on board. But what I felt for many years as a younger, angrier, more powerless person was that *Titanic* really was a 'rich person's tragedy'; that it was about the powerful and wealthy perishing or surviving in opulent surroundings. This is reflected in most of the popular representations of *Titanic* in the last century. Most dramatizations of the sinking focus not on the poor who saw *Titanic* as a Godsend at a time of great poverty, but on the powerful men and glamorous socialites of the day who lost their lives. Think of *Titanic* and you can't help but see its opulent staircase, its beautiful dining saloon, the best of everything and dripping with luxury. What doesn't spring to mind is the filthy, black boiler rooms in the very bowels of the ship; of the sleeping quarters of the workers, bunked together and sharing lavatory facilities, of the hovels and slums many of the workers came from on the day they set sail, of their illnesses, their malnourishment, the deaths in their families they'd had to endure. The focus on *Titanic* has been too long on one half of those on board and not enough on the nameless, voiceless widows of men who did backbreaking work on low pay, just to keep food on the table and to provide their children some shoes for school. It is time to remember those men and women, who had lived such hard lives since they were born, staring out into the icy north Atlantic knowing they would surely die. The world has been wonderful at remembering *Titanic*. But what people didn't see was how the great sense of loss carried on *after* the memorial services and charity events were long finished. They didn't see the longing that ordinary, working class wives and mothers and children would have had simply to have a grave and a body. This was so very needed so they could have what we'd now call 'closure' that their loved one was truly dead.

Emily was told William was not coming back when a letter arrived at her door days after the tragedy. Until that day, she had queued with hundreds of others at the White Star Line offices, hoping and praying William's name would appear on the survivors' list. She didn't give up hope. But even being told he was officially lost at sea was never enough to allow her to truly grieve in the way she needed to. Would you ever give up hope that one day, somehow, that person 'lost at sea' might just turn up on the doorstep? One hundred years ago, in a world where it was almost impossible to trace someone missing abroad, might there be a chance they'd turn up somewhere, perhaps concussed or amnesiac and alive? I know I would always have that flicker of hope, however ridiculous it might seem. Other relatives of crew who died coped and grieved in different ways. Some could speak of it, others could not. This tragedy has reverberated and echoed down the years, with many of the crew's wives unable to talk about it with their family. When their sons came of age, they too went to sea blindly because it was 'what men did'. There was no counselling, no psychological support. Off these traumatised, bereaved young men went on boats and liners, doing the same jobs as their fathers in many cases, only to always know that somewhere, deep under that ocean, their father lay unaccounted for. Unburied. Lost. No grave to mark him. The *Titanic* tragedy is still living and breathing in Southampton today. Memorials dotted around the city ensure the dead are not forgotten. You only have to ask the people who live there. The memory of *Titanic* lives on in the descendants of those who died who still feel great sadness when they speak of it. It is in the plaques on buildings around the city. It is in the buildings which featured in the background of *Titanic*'s story: the South Western House, then called the South Western Hotel, where many passengers stayed before boarding *Titanic*; the Grapes pub where many crewmembers had a last drink before boarding; and of course Canute Chambers, the building which once housed the White Star Line offices. It is in the dock area, however pristine it now is. It is on the very pavements. All these places are haunted with the ghosts of *Titanic* and the sense of loss is still very much there. It always will be.

But there is another emotion we descendants feel; pride. When my great-grandfather died, he, like many stokers, was referred to generically among family and friends as 'one of the engineers' because to be a fireman had derogatory connotations of heavy drinking and fighting. Far better to say 'engineer' and hold your head high. As a child and teenager, I too gravitated far more towards the richer passengers on board the ship whenever I saw another documentary or film adaptation. I could not imagine what life was like down in the boiler rooms and didn't really want to. That life was dirty, uncomfortable and hopeless, so I believed. And so, I turned my sympathies instead to the ermine-coated American heiresses or young English debutantes sitting wash-board straight at dinner in first class or the quiet, forgotten ones in second class or even the hopeful emigrants in steerage. Somehow, I could identify with them more; certainly far more than the crew. But of course, with age, comes a greater understanding and pathos. In time, those sympathies remained with every class of passenger on board that fateful ship, but I began to understand the struggle and desperation of those working deep in her depths, in the sweltering boiler rooms, or cleaning up after richer folk in first and second class, or preparing aristocrats' bedding for them. These people slowly became less of the fuzzy background characters I'd always imagined them to be and they began to have shape and form and substance. The workers began to become clear to me as what they truly were – not extras without speaking parts in the many films about *Titanic*, but real people with hopes and dreams and aspirations for a better life. And a fierce pride began to grow inside me. I became proud at last that my great-grandfather had taken that back-breaking job as a fireman at aged 40; that he took it eagerly to provide for his family. I began to tell people that my great-grandfather was not an engineer after all. No, my great-grandfather William Bessant was a hard and burly stoker. Likewise, the descendants who have helped me piece together their family stories for this book have told me they feel proud too. The *Titanic* workers were not only strong, tough and hard, I've come to realize. It's now time to give them adjectives that show them as more than desperate peasants who were the lowliest members of that opulent ship. I now like to use words such as proud, hard-working, hopeful, and dedicated – because that is what these workers were. From the young mothers such as widow Lucy Snape who went to sea in her first ever job to provide for her young baby, to the burly hard stokers and trimmers who'd fought with their fists for jobs at the docks to keep their families fed, to the respectable stewards with families and new brides left behind, to the fresh-faced teenage bell-boys, each and every one of the *Titanic's* crew members were real human beings with desires for no more than a better standard of living for themselves and their families. When I have spoken to relatives in the course of researching this book, these are the sentiments I get from them as well; that they are fiercely proud of their ancestors who perished or who survived and fiercely determined to preserve their memories.

Thanks to historians who compiled the crew's stories, the workers were relatively easy to find. The *Titanic* crewmen's stories have been pieced together by many historians and passionate *Titanic* researchers long before me. The women left behind, of course, were harder to source and track down. They are more elusive, silent. Many descendants of *Titanic* crew I spoke to said that the female loved ones left behind in their families didn't talk about their loss. But the women have also been forgotten because of the age in which they lived. Their grief and financial ruin happened at a time when women, particularly working-class women, had so few rights. These women had lived in poverty since their mothers before them; a long line of female silent struggle. Their daily lives are barely remembered in history. The suffrage movement is indeed documented in great depth from this era, but ordinary working-class women were not able to be so vocal. They were not able to seek rights because their poverty held them in check. Because of this, they are perceived as silent, invisible. This is why the Titanic Relief Fund minute books are so important and precious. Kept safely in the City Archives, they document these women's lives in minute detail. The 100-year-old musty-smelling pages speak of these widows' lives: their children's illnesses and successes in apprenticeships; their maternal ability or lack of it; their moving on and remarrying and finding love again or, like Emily, remaining alone for the rest of their days. Without these primary sources, we would know nothing of how the women left behind suffered but also how very stoical and brave they were in the face of adversity and hardship. Without these sources these women and their little, ordinary domestic lives would never be remembered. A quart of milk or a few eggs or 'nourishing food for a month' may seem like mundane facts to be noted and remembered when compared to the other cataclysmic events they lived through. But they are a hugely important part of social history from a time where women were held in check by society's expectations. These women's poverty and reliance on their men and their seafaring incomes show how helpless they were, not because they were 'little' women, but because that's how life was. These working-class women were dependent on men's incomes at sea. When her seaman husband died, she had nothing. No job, no help. Some took in lodgers or did charring work, but many were unable to because of illness, grief or simply being unable to know where to start. These women were living through great upheaval and thanks to the suffrage movement would soon have more rights. But for them it didn't quite come soon enough. Because of this, many remained dependent for many years, even until their dying day, on the Titanic Relief Fund and other charity – long after their husbands had drowned or been lost at sea.

But what of grief? One of the commonest replies I received from descendants of the crew during researching this book was that the remaining relatives didn't speak much of the tragedy and of their feelings. In many cases, remaining male family members often still went into seafaring occupations as their fathers had done. Many survivors too suffered in silence for the rest of their lives, unable to speak of the horrors they experienced that night. At first, from my position in my touchy-feely modern-day world of talking therapies, of the current known 'stages of grieving', of being part of a society now emotionally intelligent enough to understand that we need to discuss grief, I found this hard to comprehend. But now I do understand it. Far from being unemotional, 'low class' people, these people of 1912 felt every bit as much grief as any one of us might today if our loved one had perished on the *Titanic*. The only difference is, we would have the luxury of *time* to grieve. They did not. My aunt, whose mother was six when her father William died on *Titanic*, tells me that 'no one spoke about how they felt'. I wondered at first if I came from a family of hard sociopaths, unable to discuss their feelings. But my research only led me to find that so many other families carried on in the same way. Grieving – and being able to stop long enough to grieve – was a luxury only the rich could afford. For working class families, life carried on immediately. Bills had to be paid, stomachs filled, jobs sourced. There was no time to lament your lost love, to talk about how you were feeling, to lie in bed sobbing. You had to pay your rent or find new lodgings. You had to somehow retrieve your children's boots from the pawn shop. Was this why whenever I saw my great-grandmother's face in the family portrait taken a few years after William's death, I always found her gaze so hard, cold and steely? Was this the façade she put on for the children and the neighbours because that is what working people did? Did she ever confide in a friend how wretched she felt? Did she cry at night into her pillow? I will never know. This was not a time or a class for poetry and lamentation about grief, only for carrying on and facing the next day and all its harsh realities. Perhaps this is the reason the sorrow and empathy we all feel about those who perished on *Titanic* and their relatives is so often reserved for the rich; the clean; the eloquent. They could write or talk about their feelings and emotions. They had both the time and the money to be able to do so. Over the years, this has become a rich person's tragedy because it was the only rich voices that could be heard. Whereas for those who had to take in washing because their dead husband's wages had suddenly stopped, or for those who were made homeless and forced to sell their furniture and move into empty lodgings because they could no longer pay the rent, their emotional wellbeing took a backseat. Survival was all that mattered. Tears would not put bread on the table. Is this the reason that the voices of working-class widows, children and other dependants have been silent for so long? Popular representations of *Titanic* have been wonderful at keeping the sadness and sheer scale of the loss of the tragedy in the world's minds, but the focus has mostly been on the famous names. Where were the films of how the poor reacted to the news? Where are their stories of survival? They are there, plain to see, but they are not mainstream. They are in a handful of books or locked away in the archives in the Titanic Relief Fund minute books. Their stories are there in vivid colour with all their complexities, sadness, grief, loss, death and birth and remarriage. But on the whole, they have not been told.

Another reason that the relatives have been silent for so long is simply because they often carried on quietly. Yes, there are the cases of women who were caught drinking alcohol or women who could no longer care for their children or who were reported to the Fund for their unsatisfactory lifestyles. But, on the whole, these wives and mothers and children carried on quietly because they had endured hardship all their lives; they were used to it. The press of the day did wonders to highlight just how destitute these families were sure to become when the news first broke that their men had died. But as time passed, as expected, the world forgot about them. Although the last Titanic Relief Fund meeting was in 1959, the world's press began to stop referring to the widows and children of the tragedy. These people had always lived hand to mouth, in often slum-like conditions, pawning their possessions for another day's grace and a bit of breathing space. As time passed, was their hardship really newsworthy anymore? Just two years after *Titanic* sank, the most horrific world war began, its deaths and sheer huge numbers of those missing or injured eclipsed the stories of the women and children carrying on without their seamen husbands. As a journalist who works for national newspapers and magazines, I know all too well how important it is that a story is 'fresh' and trending.

As the years passed although anniversaries of the *Titanic*'s sinking were marked, the readers of the national and international press forgot those widows and children. J.J. Astor and Benjamin Guggenheim would always be remembered for dying 'as men should'. But would a faceless, nameless stoker or trimmer? As a result of the anonymous working-class crewmen disappearing from history's memory, so did their widows and children. Fifty years passed, then one hundred. Blockbuster films were released, endless books. But really, what do we think of when we think of *Titanic*? We think of the most beautiful ship ever built with the most opulent interiors, sailing calmly into the horizon on calm seas before our minds remind us of her true fate; broken, pierced, snapped in half and now at the bottom of the ocean. Her beautiful, famous stairwell is more recognisable than the work-weary face of a humble, soot-smeared stoker. Benjamin Guggenheim did indeed go down like a gentleman. But, I and other descendants of men who died on board would argue, so did our ancestors.

My great-grandmother, Emily Bessant, raised her five children on her Titanic Relief Fund award and her compensation. Her sweet shop and 'sharabang' business brought in money and all her children thrived and moved out. Her daughter Florence, my grandmother, met a man called Charles Cook and then had my aunt Doreen and my father, Derek Cook. Over the years, my father asked more and more questions about *Titanic* of his mother and began researching. When he died of cancer in 2005, he was still collecting memorabilia, newspaper cuttings and photographs. Before he became unwell, he enjoyed watching documentaries and films about *Titanic*, but he'd often talk of William and Emily and lament the fact that the working class crew and their families were so often left out of the picture. 'Does no one remember the firemen who kept the ship going with their bare hands?' he'd often grumble. 'Or how poor Emily was after William died? Where are their stories?'

My father died in 2005, long before I made plans to write this book. But his firm belief that the working-class people left behind by *Titanic* needed their voices heard made me all the more determined to write it. Although he enjoyed the many popular representations of *Titanic*, he hated anything that made light of it. I recall him becoming particularly angry over a comedy sketch which was set on the ship. 'How can they make light of something where so many people died?' he asked angrily. But the fact was, as the years pass, a tragedy becomes something distant;

something that can be made light of. Think of the many *Titanic* 'jokes' or blasé comments about icebergs or sinking ships. As a proud descendant of a faceless, forgotten fireman who died far too soon, my father didn't approve.

When Emily Bessant died in 1935, aged 61, she left £389 7s to her sons Charles William Bessant and Stanley Bessant. She passed away on April 8, just seven days before William had died on *Titanic* in 1912, 23 years earlier. She never remarried or had another relationship and never left her home in Henry Road. With all its memories, heartaches and ghosts, it might have seemed strange, but she had her family nearby, her grown-up children beginning families. As matriarch of the family – and the only parent for so many years – the family home was where she wanted to stay. After her death, her daughter Florence, my grandmother, made Emily's house her own family home where she had my aunt Doreen. My aunt recalls growing up in the house until she was aged 12 and even recalls hearing the air raids during the Second World War and running to a nearby air raid shelter. The house on that street had so many memories but the spectre of the loss on *Titanic* was always present. Still, as my aunt recalls, despite the ghosts of *Titanic* all around and in her family home, 'no one spoke about it'.

The crew of *Titanic* came from all over and it must not be forgotten that other cities such as Exeter and Belfast and Liverpool had their grief to bear too, but Southampton made up the lion's share and suffered the largest crew losses. In total, 549 crew from Southampton died on *Titanic*. Many of them had wives and children depending on them for every single penny they earned, others were young sons whose mothers never got over their loss. The SeaCity museum in Southampton tells the story of *Titanic* wonderfully, with sights and sounds from the time and oral history interviews as well as photographs and even a 'boiler room furnace' for those who wish to see how it was being a member of the Black Gang. A wall marks the dead with names and some photographs of crew who died. William's face is missing from his name on the list of the dead. If a seaman's document or signing on photo existed of him, it hasn't been found. And regular photography clearly wasn't something the Bessants could afford. But my aunt Doreen showed me a photograph of a man, hidden inside a gold locket that Emily never took off from around her neck. It is of William. Grainy. Dark. Worn. Still, you can see that William has dark hair, prominent eyebrows and a moustache. Handsome, in a rakish way. It is the only photograph of him that now survives.

A hundred years separate me and Emily. But writing this book has made me feel so very close to her. I found her grave – a lonely stone, overgrown with weeds and grass in an old cemetery in Southampton. No one visits Emily's grave anymore and I never had done. Her stone was visible, though, and the words, although faded, were legible: *Sacred to the memory of our dear mother Emily Ellen Bessant who fell asleep April 8th 1935 aged 61 years. Rest in peace.* I laid a single yellow rose for her. It was a strange feeling, standing near to where she lay after researching so much about her life and the widows like her and how they struggled to survive. As a mother myself, during the researching and writing of this book I've looked at my own children and thought long and hard how it must have been to endure what Emily went through; keeping going, buying the weekly food on a tiny budget, keeping them clothed, at school – as well as being their only parent with no father to help guide them at a time when men were truly heads of the household. I made a promise I wouldn't let my children forget all the sacrifices Emily made so her family could stay healthy, well and provided for. Now, living in the suburbs by Southampton, I often hear the big liners with their plaintive ships' horns floating over the Solent in the mist. When I hear them, usually early in the morning or late in the evening, I always think of my great-grandparents. I offer up a silent thanks to Emily for how she kept her family together through great hardship. And I think of the admiration I have for William for working so very hard for his family, his life one long struggle only to be cut short far too soon. I've often asked myself, what would they have made of me writing this book about their lives? The truth is, however much I have focused on Emily and William, my ancestors are just two people who were affected so terribly by the loss of *Titanic* among many hundreds of others affected by it; those who lost husbands, sons, brothers – and of course the families of the three female crewmembers who died too. It is my hope that this work helps in some way to bring those hundreds of others back into the world's thoughts; for these humble, nameless people to stand side by side in history with the lauded famous big names *Titanic* is so synonymous with.

It is where they deserve to be.

Epilogue

The lady behind the desk at the *Southern Daily Echo* smiled sadly as Emily completed the form and handed over her coins. Ten years had passed since that fateful day. Ten years of rites of passage, of children leaving school, of finding work, of losing work, of ups and downs, of tears and even, occasionally, laughter. She'd never thought she'd laugh again but life has a way of moving on, of closing over the dead. Emily had managed to smile and laugh again, but always with a sense of sorrow deep down and a yearning she'd never quite managed to rid herself of.

Her eldest son Charles was working in haulage now and had married. The girls had grown into young ladies. Her younger sons were still a handful, but she was proud of them. What should she have told William about the last ten years since he'd gone? There were motor cars on the road now, increasing in their number. There were more buses. Hems had got shorter and homeowners and women over 30 now had the vote. And of course, most importantly, she had lived through a horrific world war the likes of which William could never have imagined. Charles had gone to fight and had, thank God, come back safely. Would William have gone and fought in those trenches? She closed her eyes, blinked, and carried on writing on the piece of paper. Maybe she would have lost William anyway in the war? So many of her friends and neighbours had lost husbands that way. She finished writing and smiled at the lady behind the newspaper office desk.

'All done?' the lady asked.

'Yes, thank you,' Emily replied.

The woman read the text Emily had written and pursed her lips. 'Ten years,' she muttered. 'Doesn't seem possible, does it?'

Emily put her purse away and nodded. But the truth was, she didn't know. She didn't know whether it felt possible or not. Some mornings she'd wake up, forget, reach for William next to her and then the realisation would hit her like a brick falling onto her chest. Other days she'd have to struggle to remember what he looked like, the curve of his eyebrows, the colour of his hair or how he used to laugh. Did it feel like ten years or did it feel like yesterday? That depended on the moment, the hour, the second.

Job done, she thanked the lady and turned and walked out of the newspaper office and down the steps onto the street outside. It was sunny but with the threat of April rains as usual. She remembered that day ten years earlier when she'd stood at the docks with the children, all waving madly at a great big ship with yellow funnels, hoping a man they couldn't see might see them in the crowds of tens of thousands. She stopped then, suddenly back in 1912. If she'd known...if she'd known would she have pushed her way through the crowds, through the guards at the docks, onto that ship and down the stairwells into the boiler rooms? If she'd known, would she have barred Will's way that very morning so he couldn't have left the safety of their home?

Back inside the newspaper building, the clerk typed up the memorial Emily had just requested for the paper in a few days' time. It would appear in the Southern Daily Echo on 15 April 1922, on the tenth anniversary of *Titanic*'s loss. It read:

In loving memory of Will, beloved husband of Emily Ellen Bessant, of 5 Henry Road, Freemantle, who was lost at sea on April 15th 1912 – Deeply missed by his loving wife and children. Ten years have passed but to memory ever dear...

Notes

Chapter 1

1. Jemima, Sheila; *Chapel and Northam: An Oral History of Southampton's Dockland Communities 1900-1945*; p 72
2. *Southampton Times and Hampshire Express*, 13 April 1912, p3
3. *The Southern Daily Echo*, Saturday March 9, 1912
4. Jemima, Sheila; *Chapel and Northam: An Oral History of Southampton's Dockland Communities 1900-1945*; p 72
5. De Kerbrech, Richard P; *Down Amongst the Black Gang, The World and Workplace of RMS Titanic's Stokers*: p112
6. Anstey, Christine M; *A History of the Southampton Technical College Buildings, formerly the workhouse, with special attention to architecture; the author, 1978*
7. De Kerbrech, Richard P; p111
8. *Southern Daily Echo*, June 17, 1911
9. *Southampton Times and Hampshire Express*, 3 June 1911
10. Hyslop, Donald, Forsyth, Alastair, Jemima, Sheila; *Titanic* Voices, Memories from the Fateful Voyage, p 46
11. *Southampton Times and Hampshire Express,* 6 April 1912m p 10
12. *Southampton Times and Hampshire Express* April 13, 1912, p 7

Chapter 2

1. Jemima, Sheila; p76
2. Ibid. p41
3. Ibid. p52
4. Ibid.
5. Southampton City Heritage Oral History
6. Jemima, Sheila; p18
7. Southampton Local Studies Group; *Hill, the Polygon and Freemantle: A Series Of Extracts,notes and Personal Reminiscences,with an Historical Introduction*, p91
8. *Suburbs of Southampton, book 5, Hill, the Polygon and Freemantle: A Series of Personal Reminiscences, Historical Notes and Memories*

NOTES

Chapter 3

1. *Southern Daily Echo*, April 1912
2. Western District Girls' School Log Book
3. Jemima, Sheila; p87
4. *Daily Mail*, 23 April 1912
5. Jemima, Sheila; p84
6. Northam Girls' School Log Book
7. 'The Deathless Story of the *Titanic*', *Lloyds Weekly News*, p 26
8. Strange, Julie-Marie; *Death, Grief and Poverty in Britain, 1870-1914*, p31
9. Letter from board of Trade, provided by descendant Mike Knowlton and released with kind permission from SeaCity Museum, Southampton County Council
10. *Hampshire Independent* 1912
11. 'The Deathless Story of the *Titanic*', *Lloyds Weekly News*, p26
12. *Southern Daily Echo*, 29 April 1912

Chapter 4

1. 'Wreck of the *Titanic*', *The War Cry*, 27 April 1912 - The Salvation Army International Heritage Centre
2. With thanks to the late Brian Ticehurst who compiled this information from White Star Line (1912) Records of Bodies and Effects (Passengers and Crew S.S *Titanic*) Recovered by Cable Steamer *MacKay Bennett*, Including Bodies Buried at Sea and Bodies Delivered at Morgue in Halifax, Nova Scotia. Public Archives of Nova Scotia, Halifax, NS.
3. Titanic Relief Fund minutes, 4 December 1912, p23-24
4. Titanic Relief Fund minutes, 29 Jan 1914, p 73
5. Titanic Relief Fund minutes, pre December 1915, p20-21
6. The Titanic Relief Scheme, Mansion House Committee, 19 March 1913
7. Titanic Relief Fund minutes, 2 March 1914
8. Titanic Relief Fund minutes, 13 December 1918, p198
9. Titanic Relief Minutes, 4 December 1912, p 23-24
10. Titanic Relief Fund minutes, 19 June 1914
11. Titanic Relief Fund minutes, 23 April 1914, p98
12. Titanic Relief Fund minutes, 15 July 1913, p43
13. Titanic Relief Fund minutes 23 April 1914, p94
14. Titanic Relief Fund minutes, 8 March, 1918, p87
15. Titanic relief Fund Minutes, 17 September 1915, p140
16. Titanic Relief Fund minutes 5 December 1912, p23-4
17. Titanic relief fund 29 January 1914, p74
18. Titanicinquiry.org

Chapter 5

1. Titanic Relief Fund minutes, Book 2 p16
2. Titanic Relief Fund minutes, Book 2 p19
3. Titanic Relief Fund minutes Book 2 p25
4. Jemima, Sheila; Chapel and Northam: An Oral History of Southampton's Dockland Communities 1900-1945, p87
5. Titanic Relief Fund minutes, 2 March 1914, p81
6. Titanic Relief Fund minutes, 29 January 1914, p71
7. Titanic Relief Fund minutes, 23 April 1914, p 96
8. Titanic Relief Fund minutes Book 2
9. *Leamington Spa Courier*, 26 April 1912
10. Titanic Relief Fund minutes, 28 May 1914, p 101
11. 'Women and Drink in Edwardian England' – *CHA Historical Papers*, Vol. 20, No 1, 1985, p119
12. Titanic Relief Fund minutes Book 2
13. Dolling Memorial Home Annual Report 1904, p 10 West Sussex County Council Library Service
14. Dolling Memorial Home Annual Report 1904, West Sussex County Council Library Service
15. Dolling Memorial Home Annual Report 1904, p4, West Sussex County Council Library Service
16. http://www.nationalarchives.gov.uk/titanic/stories/frederick-woodford.htm
17. City Heritage oral history
18. https://www.dailymail.co.uk/news/article-4261550/Bodies-class-Titanic-passengers-tossed-overboard.html
19. Titanic Relief Fund minutes 23 April 1914, p93
20. Titanic Relief Fund minutes 28 May, 1914
21. Titanic Relief Fund minutes 15 July 1913
22. Titanic Relief Fund minutes, November 28 1912

Chapter 6

1. *Southampton Times and Hampshire Express*, 27 April 1912
2. www.telegraph.co.uk/history/titanic-anniversary/9202821/Titanic-survivors-vindicated-at-last.html
3. Titanic Relief Fund minutes, Book 2, p36, 1912

Chapter 7

1. Titanic Relief Fund minutes, Book 2, p92
2. Titanic Relief Fund minutes, Book 2, 28 May, 1914, p100
3. Titanic Relief Fund minutes, Book 2, 23 April 1914 p92
4. Titanic Relief Fund minutes, Book 2, 19 June 1914, p105

5. Titanic Relief Fund minutes, Book 2, p106
6. Titanic Relief Fund minutes, Book 2, p203
7. Titanic Relief Fund minutes Book 2, p137
8. Titanic Relief Fund minutes, Book 2, 23 April 1914
9. Titanic Relief Fund minutes Book 2, 27, October 1913, p57
10. Letter in loose papers Titanic Relief Fund Book 2, 11 December 1926
11. Jemima, Sheila, p89
12. Titanic Relief Fund minutes, Book 3, p59
13. Titanic Relief Fund minutes

Chapter 8
1. Titanic Relief Fund minutes, Book 3, 1 September 1942,
2. Titanic Relief Fund minutes, Book 3, 1 September 1942,
3. Titanic Relief Fund minutes, Book 3, 5 March 1946, p66
4. Titanic Relief Fund minutes, Book 3, 4 March 1947, p89
5. (Titanic Relief Fund minutes, Book 3, 7 January 1947, p86
6. Titanic Relief Fund minutes, Book 3. 3 September 1946, p79
7. Titanic Relief Fund minutes, Book 3, 2 September 1947, p95
8. Titanic Relief Fund minutes, Book 3, 12 April, 1949, p121
9. Titanic Relief Fund minutes Book 3, 7 September, 1948
10. Titanic Relief Fund minutes Book 3, 5 July 1942, p126
11. titanicinquiry.org
12. Titanic Relief Fund minutes, Book 3, 6 March 1956
13. Titanic Relief Fund minutes, Book 3, 29 August 1957
14. Titanic Relief Fund minutes, Book 3, 28 November 1957
15. Titanic Relief Fund minutes, Book3, p192
16. Titanic Relief Fund minutes, Book 3
17. Titanic Relief Fund minutes, Book 3
18. 'The Deathless Story of the *Titanic*,' *Lloyds Weekly News*, p39
19. Documents of the 1913-1914 Conference on Safety of Life at Sea: Committee on Life Saving Appliances
20. Text of the Convention for the Safety of Life at Sea. Signed at London, January 20, 1914, Open Library
21. Text of the Convention for the Safety of Life at Sea. Signed at London, January 20, 1914, Open Library

Chapter 9
1. 'The Deathless Story of the *Titanic*', *Lloyds Weekly News*, p4

Bibliography

Anstey, Christine M; *A History of the Southampton Technical College Buildings, Formerly the Workhouse, with special attention to architecture*, the author, 1978;

Archibold, Rick and McCauley, Dana; *Last Dinner on the* Titanic, Madison Press Ltd and Rick Archibold, 1997;

Gibbs, Philip; 'The Deathless Story of the *Titanic*', *Lloyds Weekly News*, 1912;

Gregson, Sarah; 'Women and Children First? The Administration of Titanic Relief in Southampton 1912-1959'; *The English Historical Review*, Volume CXXVII

Hyslop, Donald, Forsyth, Alastair, Jemima, Sheila; *Titanic Voices, Memories from the Fateful Voyage*, Southampton City Council, 1994

Jemima, Sheila; *Chapel and Northam, An Oral History of Southampton's Dockland Communities, 1900-1954*, Southampton: Oral History, Southampton City Council, 1991.

Local Studies Group; *Hill, the Polygon and Freemantle, A series of personal reminiscences historical notes and memories (Suburbs of Southampton, book 5)* Southampton, 1985

Lord, Walter; *A Night To Remember*, London: Penguin, 1978

de Kerbrech, Richard P; *Down Amongst the Black Gang: The World and Workplace of RMS* Titanic's *Stokers,* Stroud: The History Press, 2014;

Raffo, Eric H; *Half a Loaf: the care of the sick and poor in South Stoneham 1664-1948,* Friends of Moorgreen Hospital, 2000;

Strange, Julie-Marie; *Death, Grief and Poverty in Britain 1870-1914*, Cambridge University Press, 2005;

Ticehurst, Brian; Titanic*; Southampton's Memorials*, Waterfront, 1987

Ticehurst, Brian J; *The Crew of the RMS* Titanic*: Who were they?* Southampton City Council, 2006

Ticehurst, Brian J; Titanic's *Memorials World-wide: where they are located: a listing of the memorials and grave sites/stones of both* Titanic *victims and survivors,* Southampton: B &J Printers, 2006

Wilkinson, Michael and Hamilton, Robert; *The Story of the Unsinkable* Titanic, Transatlantic Press, 2011;

Wright, David and Chorniawry, Cathy, *Women and Drink in Edwardian England*, The Canadian Historical Association, 1985

Websites:

https://www.britishtitanicsociety.com/
http://www.nationalarchives.gov.uk/
https://www.encyclopedia-titanica.org

Newspapers:

Southern Daily Echo
Daily Mail
Hampshire Advertiser
Hampshire Independent
The Daily Sketch
Daily Graphic
Lloyds Weekly News
The Daily Sketch

Film:

A Night to Remember, directed by Roy Ward Baker
Titanic, written and directed by James Cameron

Index